T0368394

Heavenly Key
A Collection of 100
Heart-opening Verses
of the Holy Quran

HEAVENLY KEY
A COLLECTION OF 100
HEART-OPENING VERSES
OF THE HOLY QURAN

KHAWAR YAQUB

authorHOUSE'

AuthorHouse™
1663 Liberty Drive
Bloomington, IN 47403
www.authorhouse.com
Phone: 833-262-8899

Published by AuthorHouse 11/21/2024

ISBN: 979-8-8230-3686-3 (sc)
ISBN: 979-8-8230-3687-0 (e)

Library of Congress Control Number: 2024923368

Print information available on the last page.

Any people depicted in stock imagery provided by Getty Images are models, and such images are being used for illustrative purposes only. Certain stock imagery © Getty Images.

This book is printed on acid-free paper.

Índice

REFERENCIAS DE LAS ORACIONES:

REFERENCIAS DE LOS 20 MEJORES VERSÍCULOS DEL SAGRADO CORÁN PARA CRISTIANOS

REFERENCIAS DE LOS PÁRRAFOS:

بِسْمِ ٱللَّهِ ٱلرَّحْمَٰنِ ٱلرَّحِيمِ

En el nombre de Alá, el Compasivo, el Misericordioso.

In the name of Allah, the Compassionate, the Merciful.

I seek refuge with Allah from the accursed Satan.
In the name of Allah, The Compassionate, The Merciful.

My name is Khawar Yaqub (Pronounced Ya-coob). I was born in Pakistan and came to America at the age of twenty-four. In my forty-seven year of life thus far, I have had many experiences that shaped the man I am today and I am blessed to be able to share some of the wisdom that has been shared with me.

When the vision to create this book was given to me, I felt that it was important to share my history with you in hopes that you can my personal journey in the hope that it inspires you to do the same.

During my school life in-between the seventh and tenth grades, I would accompany my younger sister and read the Holy Quran in Arabic. Seeing as my national language is Urdu and my mother tongue is Punjabi, this task took me three years to complete.

While in school, I would cut out quotes from newspapers. Assemble them on pieces of paper, make copies and give them to my friends. To extend knowledge to those I cared for was something that always felt natural to me.

In college, I joined a professional soccer team. With my earnings, I would buy beautiful quality Qurans and gift them to my friends. After winning a bronze medal in the national games of Pakistan, I came to America. I started working 6pm to 6 am, 12 hour per day, seven days a week at a gas station.

One day, a thought came to my mind after taking three years to read the Holy Quran in Arabic, I didn't know a single sentence of what was written because I didn't understand the Arabic language!

So in the year 2000, I started reading the Holy Quran in Urdu to understand its meaning fully.

One day, while working, I found a book in the trash. When I retrieved it, I discovered that it was the Holy Bible, I gifted that book to a Christian because at the time I didn't know English very well. After a month or so, a kind person gave me the Holy Bible translated in Urdu. In the last twenty years, I have been able to study the Holy Quran and the Holy Bible in Urdu which helped with my understanding of the holy text and its meaning.

Never in my wildest dreams did I think that a childhood journey would lead to choosing the one-hundred best verses of the Holy Quran. It was put in my heart to do this good deed before going to the Lord. Therefore by the grace of the Lord, I have compiled this book in the hopes that it becomes easier and less of a daunting task for people to know and study the Holy Quran.

If even a single person in the whole world reads my book, or even a single verse enters the heart of a single persons, that will be enough for me. Knowing I helped them draw near and have a better understanding of the holy text was my intention for this book. My hopes are that by reading this Book, it allows the reader to increase their knowledge as much as possible in a short time frame. Indeed, all the verses of the Holy Quran are holy and great. I encourage you to read every verse of the Holy Quran by yourself in your favorite language. What started as a project for myself, based on the goal to help others, for inspiration for the reader to take.

May Allah create in your heart the desire to read, understand and act on the book of Allah. May you understand the purpose of life and may your life be in accordance with His commands. May Allah include you among His righteous people.

May the goal of your life be that Allah is pleased with you. May He forgive all our sins without punishment and reckoning and by His grace and mercy, may I and yourself be included among His righteous servants.

Amen.

Thank you for taking time to read this collection of verses. I sincerely hope that there are many people in the world who will understand the call to add to this library of knowledge and I am blessed to help start the conversation. I feel that this is the start of a journey that I have been called to be a part of. I am eternally grateful for this opportunity and am thankful to those that have been helpful in my life.

Sincerely,
Khawar Yaqub

In the name of Allah the most Beneficent, the most Merciful

In the Holy Qur'an, the Lord of all the worlds has commanded that by reading the book which has been revealed to you and observing prayer, surely prayer prevents sins and the remembrance of Allah is a great thing (29:45).

O you who believe, remember Allah often (33:41)

Those who remember Allah standing, sitting, and lying down, and are concerned about the creation of the heavens and the earth, say, "O our Lord, You have not created all this in vain, and are free from all defects, so save us from the punishment of Hellfire." (3:191)

Allah created jinn and man only for His worship (51:56)

Allah created death and life to test you as to which of you is good in deeds, and Allah is Mighty, Forgiving (67:02)

If We had sent down the Holy Qur'an on a mountain, the mountain would have bowed and burst in fear of Allah (59:21)

It is written in Sahih al-Bukhari's Hadith No. 5028 that Prophet Mohammad (peace be upon him) said, "The best of you are those who learn and teach the Holy Qur'an."

In the Holy Qur'an, the Lord of the Universe says: Remember Me, I will remember you, be the thankful to Me and do not be ungrateful to Me (2:152).

Allah took you out of you mothers' wombs while you knew nothing and gave you ears, eyes and hearts so that you may thank Allah (16:78)

No one is given an old age, nor is his age shortened (35:11)

Remember the name of your Lord and turn your attention to Allah alone (73:08).

And put your trust in the living Lord who will never die. Glorify and praise Allah, and He is well aware of the sins of His servants (58:25).

Allah is ever-living, there is no god but Allah, so call upon Him, worshipping Him in particular. All praise is due to Allah, the Sustainer of all the worlds (40:65).

Satan took Jesus Christ the son of Mary to a very high mountain and showed him all the kingdoms of the world and their glory.

Jesus Christ the son of Mary, (peace be upon him) said to him, O Satan, be far away, for it is written that you shall worship the Lord your God and worship Him alone. (ST. MATTHEW 4:8, 9, 10)

One of the jurists asked Jesus Christ the son of Mary, peace be upon him, which is the first commandment among all commandments.

Jesus Christ the son of Mary (peace be upon him) replied that the first commandment is: O Israel, listen: The Lord our God is one Lord, and you shall love the Lord your God with all your heart and with all your soul and with all your mind and with all your strength. (ST. MARK 12: 28, 29, 30)

O Lord of the whole universe! Forgive us all our sins without reckoning without punishment with your grace and mercy and purify us and the hearts and souls of our generations until the Day of Resurrection.

Protect us and the hearts and souls of our generations from Satan until the Day of Resurrection.

O Holy Lord of all the worlds! Fill the lives and homes of us and our generations with your mercy and grace until the Day of Judgement.

O Holy Lord of all the worlds! Fill the lives and homes of us and our generations with faith and guidance until the Day of Resurrection.

O Holy Lord of all the worlds! May the lives and homes of us and our generations be filled with health, blessings and peace til the Day of Judgement, Amen.

Me llamo Khawar Yaqub (Jacob).

Nací en Pakistán y vine a Estados Unidos a los 24 años y ahora tengo 47 años.

Entre el 7º y el 10º año de escuela, todos los días, antes de ir a la escuela, solía ir con mi hermana menor a leer el Sagrado Corán en árabe. En tres años, aprendí a leer el Sagrado Corán en árabe, mientras que mi lengua materna es el punjabi y la lengua nacional es el Urdu.

En la escuela, recortaba citas de los periódicos, las juntaba en un papel, hacía copias y se las daba a mis amigos.

En mi vida universitaria, me uní a un equipo de fútbol profesional y solía comprar bonitos Coranes de calidad con pendientes de fútbol y regalárselos a mis amigos.

Después de ganar una medalla de bronce en los juegos nacionales de Pakistán, vine a Estados Unidos y empecé a trabajar de seis a doce horas al día, siete días a la semana en una estación de gasolina.

Un día me vino a la mente el pensamiento de que después de 3 años de leer el Sagrado Corán en árabe, no sabía ni una sola frase de

lo que estaba escrito en el Sagrado Corán,
porque no entendía la lengua árabe.
En 2000, empecé a leer el Sagrado Corán en
urdu para entenderlo.
Un día, cuando estaba en el trabajo, encontré
un libro en la basura y, cuando lo saqué,
estaba escrito en él la Santa Biblia.
Regalé ese libro a un cristiano, porque no
entendía el inglés.
Al cabo de un mes, una persona me regaló la
Santa Biblia en Urdu, así que en los últimos
20 años sólo he estudiado el Sagrado Corán y
la Santa Biblia.
Nunca pensé que este viaje de mi infancia me
llevaría a elegir los 100 mejores versículos del
Sagrado Corán. Quiero hacer algunas buenas
acciones antes de ir al Señor. Por lo tanto, por
la gracia del Señor, he compilado este libro,
para que sea fácil para la gente conocer el
Sagrado Corán.
Si una sola persona en todo el mundo lee mi
libro, o un solo verso entra en el corazón de
una sola persona, será suficiente para mí:
tanto si alguien lo lee como si no, yo mismo
leeré este libro hasta que muera e intentaré
actuar de acuerdo con él.

Si Dios quiere, la paz y la gracia del Señor
sean con todos vosotros, Amén.

¡Gracias!

En el nombre de Alá, el Compasivo, el Misericordioso.

بِسْمِ ٱللَّهِ ٱلرَّحْمَٰنِ ٱلرَّحِيمِ

En el Sagrado Corán, el Señor de todos los mundos ha ordenado que, al leer el libro que te ha sido revelado y observar la oración, ciertamente la oración previene los pecados y el recuerdo de Allah es una gran cosa (29:45).

Oh vosotros que creéis, recordad a Allah a menudo (33:41).

Aquellos que recuerdan a Allah de pie, sentados y acostados, y están preocupados por la creación de los cielos y la tierra, dicen: "Nuestro Señor, no has creado todo esto en vano. Estás libre de todos los defectos, así que sálvanos del castigo del Infierno." (3:191)

Allah creó a los genios y a los hombres solo para Su adoración (51:56).

Allah creó la muerte y la vida para probar cuál de vosotros es mejor en obras, y Allah es Poderoso, Perdonador (67:02).

Si hubiéramos hecho descender el Sagrado Corán sobre una montaña, la montaña se habría inclinado y estallado por el temor de Allah (59:21).

Está escrito en el Hadiz No. 5028 de Sahih al-Bukhari que el Profeta Muhammad (que la paz sea con él) dijo: "Los mejores entre vosotros son aquellos que aprenden y enseñan el Sagrado Corán."

En el Sagrado Corán, el Señor del Universo dice: "Recordadme, que Yo os recordaré. Sed agradecidos conmigo y no seáis ingratos" (2:152).

Allah os sacó de los vientres de vuestras madres sin que supierais nada, y os dio oídos, ojos y corazones para que pudierais agradecer a Allah (16:78).

A nadie se le da una vejez, ni se acorta su vida (35:11).

Recordad el nombre de vuestro Señor y volved vuestra atención solo a Allah (73:08).

Y confiad en el Señor viviente que nunca morirá. Glorificad y alabad a Allah, y Él está bien consciente de los pecados de Sus siervos (58:25).

Allah es siempre viviente, no hay más dios que Allah, así que llamadle, adorándole a Él en particular. Toda alabanza es para Allah, el Sustentador de todos los mundos (40:65).

El diablo llevó a Jesús a una montaña muy alta y le mostró todos los reinos del mundo y su gloria, y el diablo dijo: "si te postras y me adoras, te daré todo."

Jesucristo dijo: "¡Oh Satanás, aléjate, porque está escrito que adorarás al Señor tu Dios y solo a Él adorarás!" (San Mateo 4:8, 9, 10).

Uno de los juristas preguntó a Jesucristo cuál es el mandamiento primero de todos. Jesucristo respondió: "Escucha, Israel, el Señor nuestro Dios, el Señor es uno, y amarás al Señor tu Dios con todo tu corazón, con toda tu alma, con toda tu mente y con todas tus fuerzas" (San Marcos 12:28, 29, 30).

Oh Santo Señor de todos los mundos, protégenos a nosotros y a nuestras generaciones del Satanás, concédenos la oportunidad de hacer el bien y evitar el mal, concédenos la oportunidad de aprender de nuestros errores y las virtudes de los demás, perdona nuestros pecados con tu gracia y misericordia, e ilumina los hogares de todos con tu misericordia, gracia, guía, fe, salud, bendiciones y paz.

Oh Santo Señor de todos los mundos, protégenos a nosotros y a nuestras generaciones de Satanás, concédenos la oportunidad de hacer el bien y evitar el mal, concédenos la oportunidad de aprender de nuestras faltas y de las virtudes de los demás, perdona nuestros pecados con tu gracia y misericordia, e

ilumina los hogares de todos con tu misericordia y gracia, guía, fe, salud, bendiciones
y paz.
Oh Santo Señor de todos los mundos, protégenos a nosotros y a los corazones y almas
de nuestras generaciones de Satanás hasta el
Día del Juicio.
Oh Santo Señor de todos los mundos, purifí-
canos a nosotros y a los corazones y almas
de nuestras generaciones hasta el Día de la
Resurrección.

Amén.

Referencias De Los 100 Mejores Versículos Del Sagrado Corán

SURAH 6, VERSO 162

قُلْ إِنَّ صَلَاتِي وَنُسُكِي وَمَحْيَايَ وَمَمَاتِي لله رَبِّ ٱلْعَٰلَمِينَ

Di: "En verdad, mi oración, mis ritos de sacrificio, mi vivir y mi morir son para Alá, Señor de los mundos."

Say, "Indeed, my prayer, my rites of sacrifice, my living and my dying are for Allah, Lord of the worlds."

Surah 51, Verso 56

وَمَا خَلَقْتُ ٱلْجِنَّ وَٱلْإِنسَ إِلَّا لِيَعْبُدُونِ

No he creado a los genios ni a los hombres sino para que Me adoren.

And I did not create the jinn and mankind except to worship Me.

Surah 2, Verso 152

فَٱذْكُرُونِيٓ أَذْكُرْكُمْ وَٱشْكُرُواْ لِي وَلَا تَكْفُرُونِ

**Acordaos de Mí y Yo me acordaré de vosotros.
Agradecedme y no Me neguéis.**

*So remember Me; I will remember you. And be grateful to
Me and do not deny Me.*

SURAH 14, VERSO 7

وَإِذْ تَأَذَّنَ رَبُّكُمْ لَئِن شَكَرْتُمْ لَأَزِيدَنَّكُمْ وَلَئِن كَفَرْتُمْ إِنَّ عَذَابِي لَشَدِيدٌ

Y [recuerda] cuando tu Señor proclamó: 'Si eres agradecido, ciertamente te incrementaré [en favor]; pero si reniegas, ciertamente, Mi castigo es severo'".

And [remember] when your Lord proclaimed, 'If you are grateful, I will surely increase you [in favor]; but if you deny, indeed, My punishment is severe.'"

SURAH 6, VERSO 120

وَذَرُواْ ظَاهِرَ ٱلْإِثْمِ وَبَاطِنَهُۥٓ إِنَّ ٱلَّذِينَ يَكْسِبُونَ ٱلْإِثْمَ سَيُجْزَوْنَ بِمَا كَانُواْ يَقْتَرِفُونَ

Y dejad lo aparente del pecado y lo oculto del mismo. Ciertamente, quienes se ganan [la culpa por] el pecado serán recompensados por lo que solían cometer.

And leave what is apparent of sin and what is concealed thereof. Indeed, those who earn [blame for] sin will be recompensed for that which they used to commit.

SURAH 2, VERSO 153

يَـٰٓأَيُّهَا ٱلَّذِينَ ءَامَنُوا۟ ٱسْتَعِينُوا۟ بِٱلصَّبْرِ وَٱلصَّلَوٰةِ إِنَّ ٱللَّهَ مَعَ ٱلصَّـٰبِرِينَ

Oh vosotros que habéis creído, buscad ayuda mediante la paciencia y la oración. Alah está con los pacientes.

O you who have believed, seek help through patience and prayer. Indeed, Allah is with the patient.

SURAH 17, VERSO 111

وَقُلِ ٱلْحَمْدُ للَّهِ ٱلَّذِي لَمْ يَتَّخِذْ وَلَدًا وَلَمْ يَكُن لَّهُ شَرِيكٌ فِى ٱلْمُلْكِ وَلَمْ يَكُن لَّهُ
وَلِىٌّ مِّنَ ٱلذُّلِّ وَكَبِّرْهُ تَكْبِيرًا

**Y decid: "Alabado sea Alá, que no ha tomado hijo y no
ha tenido compañero en [Su] dominio y no tiene
[necesidad de un] protector por debilidad; y
glorificadle con [gran] glorificación."**

*And say, "Praise to Allah, who has not taken a son and has
had no partner in [His] dominion and has no [need of a]
protector out of weakness; and glorify Him with [great]
glorification."*

SURAH 4, VERSO 48

إِنَّ ٱللَّهَ لَا يَغْفِرُ أَن يُشْرَكَ بِهِۦ وَيَغْفِرُ مَا دُونَ ذَٰلِكَ لِمَن يَشَآءُ وَمَن يُشْرِكْ بِٱللَّهِ فَقَدِ ٱفْتَرَىٰ إِثْمًا عَظِيمًا

Ciertamente, Alá no perdona la asociación con Él, pero perdona lo que es menos que eso a quien Él quiere. Y quien asocia a otros con Alá, ciertamente ha fabricado un pecado tremendo.

Indeed, Allah does not forgive association with Him, but He forgives what is less than that for whom He wills. And he who associates others with Allah has certainly fabricated a tremendous sin.

SURAH 40, VERSO 55

فَٱصْبِرْ إِنَّ وَعْدَ ٱللَّهِ حَقٌّ وَلَا يَسْتَخِفَّنَّكَ ٱلَّذِينَ لَا يُوقِنُونَ

Tened, pues, paciencia, pues la promesa de Alah es verdad. Y que no te inquieten quienes no están seguros [en la fe].

So be patient, indeed, the promise of Allah is truth. And let them not disquiet you who are not certain [in faith].

SURAH 33, VERSO 36

وَمَا كَانَ لِمُؤْمِنٍ وَلَا مُؤْمِنَةٍ إِذَا قَضَى ٱللَّهُ وَرَسُولُهُۥٓ أَمْرًا أَن يَكُونَ لَهُمُ
ٱلْخِيَرَةُ مِنْ أَمْرِهِمْ وَمَن يَعْصِ ٱللَّهَ وَرَسُولَهُۥ فَقَدْ ضَلَّ ضَلَـٰلًا مُّبِينًا

**Y no corresponde al creyente, hombre o mujer, cuando
Alá y Su Enviado han decretado un asunto, que [a
partir de entonces] tenga elección sobre su asunto.
Quien desobedezca a Alá y a Su Enviado ha caído en
un error manifiesto.**

*And it is not for a believer, man or woman, when Allah and
His Messenger have decreed a matter, that they should
[thereafter] have any choice about their affair. And whoever
disobeys Allah and His Messenger has certainly strayed into
clear error.*

SURAH 4, VERSO 69

وَمَن يُطِعِ ٱللَّهَ وَٱلرَّسُولَ فَأُوْلَـٰٓئِكَ مَعَ ٱلَّذِينَ أَنْعَمَ ٱللَّهُ عَلَيْهِم مِّنَ ٱلنَّبِيِّـۧنَ وَٱلصِّدِّيقِينَ وَٱلشُّهَدَآءِ وَٱلصَّـٰلِحِينَ وَحَسُنَ أُوْلَـٰٓئِكَ رَفِيقًا

Quien obedezca a Alá y a Su Enviado estará entre aquellos a quienes Alá ha concedido el favor de los profetas, los que afirman la verdad, los mártires y los justos. Y excelentes son esos como compañeros.

And whoever obeys Allah and the Messenger - those will be with the ones upon whom Allah has bestowed favor of the prophets, the steadfast affirmers of truth, the martyrs and the righteous. And excellent are those as companions.

SURAH 32, VERSO 15

إِنَّمَا يُؤْمِنُ بِـَٔايَٰتِنَا ٱلَّذِينَ إِذَا ذُكِّرُواْ بِهَا خَرُّواْ سُجَّدًا وَسَبَّحُواْ بِحَمْدِ رَبِّهِمْ وَهُمْ لَا يَسْتَكْبِرُونَ

Sólo creen en Nuestros versículos quienes, cuando son recordados por ellos, se postran y exaltan [a Alá] con alabanzas a su Señor, y no son arrogantes.

Only those believe in Our verses who, when they are reminded by them, fall down in prostration and exalt [Allah] with praise of their Lord, and they are not arrogant.

SURAH 8, VERSO 2

إِنَّمَا ٱلْمُؤْمِنُونَ ٱلَّذِينَ إِذَا ذُكِرَ ٱللَّهُ وَجِلَتْ قُلُوبُهُمْ وَإِذَا تُلِيَتْ عَلَيْهِمْ ءَايَـٰتُهُۥ
زَادَتْهُمْ إِيمَـٰنًا وَعَلَىٰ رَبِّهِمْ يَتَوَكَّلُونَ

**Los creyentes son sólo aquellos que, cuando se
menciona a Alá, sus corazones se vuelven temerosos, y
cuando se les recitan Sus versículos, les aumenta la fe;
y en su Señor confían.**

*The believers are only those who, when Allah is mentioned,
their hearts become fearful, and when His verses are recited
to them, it increases them in faith; and upon their Lord they
rely.*

SURAH 10, VERSO 57

يَـٰٓأَيُّهَا ٱلنَّاسُ قَدْ جَآءَتْكُم مَّوْعِظَةٌ مِّن رَّبِّكُمْ وَشِفَآءٌ لِّمَا فِى ٱلصُّدُورِ وَهُدًى وَرَحْمَةٌ لِّلْمُؤْمِنِينَ

Oh humanidad, ha de llegaros instrucción de vuestro Señor y curación para lo que hay en los pechos y guía y misericordia para los creyentes.

O mankind, there has to come to you instruction from your Lord and healing for what is in the breasts and guidance and mercy for the believers.

SURAH 42, VERSO 52

وَكَذَٰلِكَ أَوْحَيْنَا إِلَيْكَ رُوحًا مِّنْ أَمْرِنَا ۚ مَا كُنتَ تَدْرِى مَا ٱلْكِتَٰبُ وَلَا ٱلْإِيمَٰنُ وَلَٰكِن جَعَلْنَٰهُ نُورًا نَّهْدِى بِهِۦ مَن نَّشَآءُ مِنْ عِبَادِنَا ۚ وَإِنَّكَ لَتَهْدِىٓ إِلَىٰ صِرَٰطٍ مُّسْتَقِيمٍ

Y así os hemos revelado una inspiración de Nuestro mandato. No sabíais lo que es el Libro ni lo que es la fe, pero hemos hecho de ella una luz por la que guiamos a quien queremos de Nuestros siervos. Y, en verdad, [Oh Muhammad], guías hacia un camino recto.

And thus We have revealed to you an inspiration of Our command. You did not know what is the Book or [what is] faith, but We have made it a light by which We guide whom We will of Our servants. And indeed, [O Muhammad], you guide to a straight path.

SURAH 34, VERSO 50

قُل إِنَّمَا أَنَا۠ بَشَرٌ مِّثْلُكُمْ يُوحَىٰ إِلَيَّ أَنَّمَا إِلَٰهُكُمْ إِلَٰهٌ وَٰحِدٌ فَمَن كَانَ
يَرْجُوا۟ لِقَآءَ رَبِّهِۦ فَلْيَعْمَلْ عَمَلًا صَٰلِحًا وَلَا يُشْرِكْ بِعِبَادَةِ رَبِّهِۦٓ أَحَدًا

Di: "No soy más que un humano como vosotros, a quien se ha revelado que vuestro dios es un solo Dios. Así pues, quien quiera esperar el encuentro con su Señor, que haga obras rectas y no asocie en la adoración de su Señor a nadie."

Say, "I am only a human like you, to whom it has been revealed that your god is one God. So whoever would hope for the meeting with his Lord - let him do righteous work and not associate in the worship of his Lord anyone."

SURAH 25, VERSO 30

وَقَالَ ٱلرَّسُولُ يَـٰرَبِّ إِنَّ قَوْمِى ٱتَّخَذُواْ هَـٰذَا ٱلْقُرْءَانَ مَهْجُورًا

Y el Mensajero ha dicho: "Oh mi Señor, ciertamente mi gente ha tomado este Corán como [una cosa] abandonada".

And the Messenger has said, "O my Lord, indeed my people have taken this Qur'an as [a thing] abandoned."

SURAH 54, VERSO 17

وَلَقَدْ يَسَّرْنَا ٱلْقُرْءَانَ لِلذِّكْرِ فَهَلْ مِن مُّدَّكِرٍ

Y, ciertamente, hemos hecho que el Corán sea fácil de recordar, así que ¿hay alguien que lo recuerde?

And We have certainly made the Qur'an easy for remembrance, so is there any who will remember?

SURAH 31, VERSO 17

يَٰبُنَىَّ أَقِمِ ٱلصَّلَوٰةَ وَأْمُرْ بِٱلْمَعْرُوفِ وَٱنْهَ عَنِ ٱلْمُنكَرِ وَٱصْبِرْ عَلَىٰ مَآ أَصَابَكَ
إِنَّ ذَٰلِكَ مِنْ عَزْمِ ٱلْأُمُورِ

**"Oh hijo mío, establece la oración, ordená-lo lo que
está bien, prohíbe lo que está mal y ten paciencia con
lo que te suceda. En verdad, [todo] eso es de los
asuntos [que requieren] determinación".**

*"O my son, establish prayer, enjoin what is right, forbid what
is wrong, and be patient over what befalls you. Indeed, [all]
that is of the matters [requiring] determination."*

SURAH 3, VERSO 104

وَلْتَكُن مِّنكُمْ أُمَّةٌ يَدْعُونَ إِلَى ٱلْخَيْرِ وَيَأْمُرُونَ بِٱلْمَعْرُوفِ وَيَنْهَوْنَ عَنِ ٱلْمُنكَرِ وَأُوْلَٰٓئِكَ هُمُ ٱلْمُفْلِحُونَ

Y que surja de vosotros una nación que invite al bien, que ordene el bien y prohíba el mal, y ésos serán los triunfadores.

And let there be [arising] from you a nation inviting to [all that is] good, enjoining what is right and forbidding what is wrong, and those will be the successful.

SURAH 49, VERSO 11

يَـٰٓأَيُّهَا ٱلَّذِينَ ءَامَنُوا۟ لَا يَسْخَرْ قَوْمٌ مِّن قَوْمٍ عَسَىٰٓ أَن يَكُونُوا۟ خَيْرًا مِّنْهُمْ وَلَا نِسَآءٌ مِّن نِّسَآءٍ عَسَىٰٓ أَن يَكُنَّ خَيْرًا مِّنْهُنَّ وَلَا تَلْمِزُوٓا۟ أَنفُسَكُمْ وَلَا تَنَابَزُوا۟ بِٱلْأَلْقَـٰبِ بِئْسَ ٱلِٱسْمُ ٱلْفُسُوقُ بَعْدَ ٱلْإِيمَـٰنِ وَمَن لَّمْ يَتُبْ فَأُو۟لَـٰٓئِكَ هُمُ ٱلظَّـٰلِمُونَ

Oh vosotros que habéis creído, no dejéis que un pueblo ridiculice a [otro] pueblo; tal vez sean mejores que ellos; ni que las mujeres ridiculicen a [otras] mujeres; tal vez sean mejores que ellas. Y no os insultéis unos a otros ni os llaméis por apodos [ofensivos]. Desdichado es el nombre de la desobediencia después de [la propia] fe. Y quien no se arrepienta, ése es el malhechor.

O you who have believed, let not a people ridicule [another] people; perhaps they may be better than them; nor let women

49

ridicule [other] women; perhaps they may be better than them. And do not insult one another and do not call each other by [offensive] nicknames. Wretched is the name of disobedience after [one's] faith. And whoever does not repent - then it is those who are the wrongdoers.

50

SURAH 49, VERSO 12

يَـٰٓأَيُّهَا ٱلَّذِينَ ءَامَنُوا۟ ٱجْتَنِبُوا۟ كَثِيرًا مِّنَ ٱلظَّنِّ إِنَّ بَعْضَ ٱلظَّنِّ إِثْمٌ وَلَا تَجَسَّسُوا۟ وَلَا يَغْتَب بَّعْضُكُم بَعْضًا أَيُحِبُّ أَحَدُكُمْ أَن يَأْكُلَ لَحْمَ أَخِيهِ مَيْتًا فَكَرِهْتُمُوهُ وَٱتَّقُوا۟ ٱللَّهَ إِنَّ ٱللَّهَ تَوَّابٌ رَّحِيمٌ

Oh vosotros que habéis creído, evitad muchas suposiciones [negativas]. En efecto, algunas suposiciones son pecado. Y no os espiéis ni os calumniéis unos a otros. ¿A alguno de vosotros le gustaría comer la carne de su hermano muerto? Lo aborreceríais. Y temed a Alá; ciertamente, Alá acepta el arrepentimiento y es misericordioso.

O you who have believed, avoid much [negative] assumption. Indeed, some assumption is sin. And do not spy or backbite each other. Would one of you like to eat the flesh of his brother when dead? You would detest it. And fear Allah; indeed, Allah is Accepting of repentance and Merciful.

SURAH 2, VERSO 44

أَتَأْمُرُونَ ٱلنَّاسَ بِٱلْبِرِّ وَتَنسَوْنَ أَنفُسَكُمْ وَأَنتُمْ تَتْلُونَ ٱلْكِتَـٰبَ أَفَلَا تَعْقِلُونَ

¿Ordenáis justicia al pueblo y os olvidáis de vosotros mismos mientras recitáis la Escritura? ¿No razonaréis entonces?

Do you order righteousness of the people and forget yourselves while you recite the Scripture? Then will you not reason?

SURAH 61, VERSO 3

كَبُرَ مَقْتًا عِندَ ٱللَّهِ أَن تَقُولُوا۟ مَا لَا تَفْعَلُونَ

Y grande es el odio a Alah que decís lo que no hacéis.

And great is the hatred of Allah that you say what you do not do.

SURAH 23, VERSE 96

اصْطَفَنكُمْ وَجَعَلَ لَكُمْ فِي الدِّينِ مِنْ حَرَجٍ ۚ مِّلَّةَ أَبِيكُمْ إِبْرَاهِيمَ ۚ هُوَ
سَمَّاكُمُ الْمُسْلِمِينَ مِن قَبْلُ وَفِي هَٰذَا لِيَكُونَ الرَّسُولُ شَهِيدًا عَلَيْكُمْ
وَتَكُونُوا شُهَدَاءَ عَلَى النَّاسِ ۚ فَأَقِيمُوا الصَّلَاةَ وَآتُوا الزَّكَاةَ وَاعْتَصِمُوا
بِاللَّهِ هُوَ مَوْلَاكُمْ ۖ فَنِعْمَ الْمَوْلَىٰ وَنِعْمَ النَّصِيرُ

**[Alá] os ha elegido y no os ha puesto en la religión
ninguna dificultad. [Es] la religión de vuestro padre,
Abraham. Alá os nombró "musulmanes" antes [en las
escrituras anteriores] y en esta [revelación] para que el
Mensajero pueda sea testigo sobre vosotros y vosotros
seáis testigos sobre la gente. Estableced la oración y
dad el zakat y aferraos a Alá. Él es vuestro protector
excelente es el Protector y excelente es el Auxiliador.**

*[Allah] has chosen you and has not placed upon you in the
religion any difficulty. [It is] the religion of your father,
Abraham. Allah named you "Muslims" before [in former*

scriptures] and in this [revelation] that the Messenger may be a witness over you and you may be witnesses over the people. So establish prayer and give zakah and hold fast to Allah. He is your protector; and excellent is the protector, and excellent is the helper.

Surah 7, Verso 199

آتْلُ مَآ أُوحِىَ إِلَيْكَ مِنَ ٱلْكِتَٰبِ وَأَقِمِ ٱلصَّلَوٰةَ إِنَّ ٱلصَّلَوٰةَ تَنْهَىٰ عَنِ ٱلْفَحْشَآءِ وَٱلْمُنكَرِ وَلَذِكْرُ ٱللَّهِ أَكْبَرُ وَٱللَّهُ يَعْلَمُ مَا تَصْنَعُونَ

Recitad lo que se os ha revelado del Libro y estableced la oración. Ciertamente, la oración prohíbe la inmoralidad y la maldad, y el recuerdo de Alá es mayor. Alá sabe lo que hacéis.

Recite what has been revealed to you of the Book and establish prayer. Indeed, prayer prohibits immorality and wrongdoing, and the remembrance of Allah is greater. And Allah knows that which you do.

Surah 6, Verso 125

فَمَن يُرِدِ ٱللَّهُ أَن يَهْدِيَهُۥ يَشْرَحْ صَدْرَهُۥ لِلْإِسْلَٰمِ وَمَن يُرِدْ أَن يُضِلَّهُۥ يَجْعَلْ صَدْرَهُۥ ضَيِّقًا حَرَجًا كَأَنَّمَا يَصَّعَّدُ فِى ٱلسَّمَآءِ كَذَٰلِكَ يَجْعَلُ ٱللَّهُ ٱلرِّجْسَ عَلَى ٱلَّذِينَ لَا يُؤْمِنُونَ

Así pues, a quien Alá quiere guiar, le ensancha el pecho para que [contenga] el Islam; y a quien quiere extraviar, le aprieta y constriñe el pecho como si subiera al cielo. Así contamina Allah a los que no creen.

So, whoever Allah wants to guide - He expands his breast to [contain] Islam; and whoever He wants to misguide - He makes his breast tight and constricted as though he were climbing into the sky. Thus does Allah place defilement upon those who do not believe.

SURAH 39, VERSO 22

فَهُوَ ٱللَّهُ ٱلْحَقُّ وَمَا يَدْعُونَ مِن دُونِهِ ٱلْبَٰطِلُ وَأَنَّ ٱللَّهَ ٱلْعَلِىُّ ٱلْكَبِيرُ

¿Así es quien [se apoya] en una prueba clara de su Señor [como la mencionada]? ¿Y le sigue un testigo de Él, y antes de él estaba el Libro de Moisés como guía y misericordia? Quienes [creen en las revelaciones anteriores] creen en él [el Corán]. Pero quien no crea en él de entre las [diversas] facciones, el Fuego es su destino prometido. No dudes de ello. Ciertamente, es la verdad de tu Señor, pero la mayoría de la gente no cree.

So is one who [stands] upon a clear evidence from his Lord [like the aforementioned]? And a witness from Him follows it, and before it was the Book of Moses as a guide and mercy? Those [believers in the former revelations] believe in it [the

Qur'an]. But whoever disbelieves in it from the [various] factions - the Fire is his promised destination. So be not in doubt about it. Indeed, it is the truth from your Lord, but most of the people do not believe.

SURAH 19, VERSO 76

وَيَزِيدُ ٱللَّهُ ٱلَّذِينَ ٱهْتَدَوْا۟ هُدًى ۗ وَٱلْبَـٰقِيَـٰتُ ٱلصَّـٰلِحَـٰتُ خَيْرٌ عِندَ رَبِّكَ ثَوَابًا وَخَيْرٌ مَّرَدًّا

Y Alah aumenta a los que fueron guiados, en guía, y las buenas acciones perdurables son mejores para tu Señor en cuanto a recompensa y mejores en cuanto a recurso.

And Allah increases those who were guided, in guidance, and the enduring good deeds are better to your Lord for reward and better for recourse.

Surah 31, Verso 18

وَلَا تُصَعِّرْ خَدَّكَ لِلنَّاسِ وَلَا تَمْشِ فِى ٱلْأَرْضِ مَرَحًا إِنَّ ٱللَّهَ لَا يُحِبُّ كُلَّ
مُخْتَالٍ فَخُورٍ

Y no pongas tu mejilla [en desprecio] hacia la gente y no andes por la tierra exultante. Ciertamente, a Alah no le gustan los autoengañados ni los jactanciosos.

And do not turn your cheek [in contempt] toward people and do not walk through the earth exultantly. Indeed, Allah does not like everyone self-deluded and boastful.

SURAH 25, VERSO 63

وَعِبَادُ ٱلرَّحْمَـٰنِ ٱلَّذِينَ يَمْشُونَ عَلَى ٱلْأَرْضِ هَوْنًا وَإِذَا خَاطَبَهُمُ ٱلْجَـٰهِلُونَ
قَالُواْ سَلَـٰمًا

Los (verdaderos) servidores del Misericordioso son aquellos que caminan humildemente sobre la tierra que, cuando la gente ignorante se comporta insolentemente con ellos, dicen: "Paz a vosotros".

The (true) servants of the Merciful are those who walk humbly on the earth who, when the ignorant people behave insolently towards them, say, "Peace to you".

Surah 64, Verso 16

فَٱتَّقُوا۟ ٱللَّهَ مَا ٱسْتَطَعْتُمْ وَٱسْمَعُوا۟ وَأَطِيعُوا۟ وَأَنفِقُوا۟ خَيْرًا لِّأَنفُسِكُمْ وَمَن يُوقَ شُحَّ نَفْسِهِۦ فَأُو۟لَٰٓئِكَ هُمُ ٱلْمُفْلِحُونَ

Temed a Alá cuanto podáis y escuchad y obedeced y gastad [en el camino de Alá]; es mejor para vosotros mismos. Quien esté protegido de la mezquindad de su alma, ése será el triunfador.

So fear Allah as much as you are able and listen and obey and spend [in the way of Allah]; it is better for your selves. And whoever is protected from the stinginess of his soul - it is those who will be the successful.

SURAH 35, VERSO 10

مَن كَانَ يُرِيدُ ٱلْعِزَّةَ فَلِلَّهِ ٱلْعِزَّةُ جَمِيعًا إِلَيْهِ يَصْعَدُ ٱلْكَلِمُ ٱلطَّيِّبُ وَٱلْعَمَلُ
ٱلصَّـٰلِحُ يَرْفَعُهُ وَٱلَّذِينَ يَمْكُرُونَ ٱلسَّيِّـَٔاتِ لَهُمْ عَذَابٌ شَدِيدٌ وَمَكْرُ أُوْلَـٰئِكَ
هُوَ يَبُورُ

Quien desee el honor [a través del poder], a Alah pertenece todo el honor. A Él asciende la buena palabra, y la obra recta la eleva. Pero los que maquinan malas acciones tendrán un castigo severo, y la maquinación de aquéllos - perecerá.

Whoever desires honor [through power] - then to Allah belongs all honor. To Him ascends good speech, and righteous work raises it. But they who plot evil deeds will have a severe punishment, and the plotting of those - it will perish.

SURAH 11, VERSO 114

وَأَقِمِ ٱلصَّلَوٰةَ طَرَفَىِ ٱلنَّهَارِ وَزُلَفًا مِّنَ ٱلَّيۡلِ إِنَّ ٱلۡحَسَنَـٰتِ يُذۡهِبۡنَ ٱلسَّيِّـَٔاتِ ذَٰلِكَ ذِكۡرَىٰ لِلذَّٰكِرِينَ

Y establece la oración en los dos extremos del día y al acercarse la noche. Ciertamente, las buenas acciones acaban con las malas. Es un recordatorio para los que recuerdan.

And establish prayer at the two ends of the day and at the approach of the night. Indeed, good deeds do away with misdeeds. That is a reminder for those who remember.

SURAH 2, VERSO 177

لَّيْسَ ٱلْبِرَّ أَن تُوَلُّواْ وُجُوهَكُمْ قِبَلَ ٱلْمَشْرِقِ وَٱلْمَغْرِبِ وَلَٰكِنَّ ٱلْبِرَّ مَنْ ءَامَنَ
بِٱللَّهِ وَٱلْيَوْمِ ٱلْءَاخِرِ وَٱلْمَلَٰٓئِكَةِ وَٱلْكِتَٰبِ وَٱلنَّبِيِّۦنَ وَءَاتَى ٱلْمَالَ عَلَىٰ حُبِّهِۦ ذَوِى
ٱلْقُرْبَىٰ وَٱلْيَتَٰمَىٰ وَٱلْمَسَٰكِينَ وَٱبْنَ ٱلسَّبِيلِ وَٱلسَّآئِلِينَ وَفِى ٱلرِّقَابِ وَأَقَامَ
ٱلصَّلَوٰةَ وَءَاتَى ٱلزَّكَوٰةَ وَٱلْمُوفُونَ بِعَهْدِهِمْ إِذَا عَٰهَدُواْ وَٱلصَّٰبِرِينَ فِى
ٱلْبَأْسَآءِ وَٱلضَّرَّآءِ وَحِينَ ٱلْبَأْسِ أُوْلَٰٓئِكَ ٱلَّذِينَ صَدَقُواْ وَأُوْلَٰٓئِكَ هُمُ ٱلْمُتَّقُونَ

No es rectitud que volváis vuestros rostros hacia el
este o el oeste, sino que la rectitud está en quien cree
en Alá, en el Último Día, en los Ángeles, en el Libro y
en los Profetas y da su riqueza, a pesar de amarla, a los
parientes, a los huérfanos, a los necesitados, al viajero,
a los que piden [ayuda] y para liberar a los esclavos; [y
quien] establece la oración y da el zakat; [quien]
cumple su promesa cuando promete; y [quien] es
paciente en la pobreza y la penuria y durante la
batalla. Ésos son los que han sido veraces, y ésos son
los justos.

It is not righteousness that you turn your faces towards the east or the west, but righteousness is in one who believes in Allah, the Last Day, the Angels, the Book, and the Prophets and gives his wealth, in spite of love for it, to relatives, orphans, the needy, the traveler, those who ask [for help], and for freeing slaves; [and who] establishes prayer and gives zakah; [those who] fulfill their promise when they promise; and [those who] are patient in poverty and hardship and during battle. Those are the ones who have been true, and it is those who are the righteous.

SURAH 33, VERSO 35

إِنَّ ٱلْمُسْلِمِينَ وَٱلْمُسْلِمَـٰتِ وَٱلْمُؤْمِنِينَ وَٱلْمُؤْمِنَـٰتِ وَٱلْقَـٰنِتِينَ وَٱلْقَـٰنِتَـٰتِ
وَٱلصَّـٰدِقِينَ وَٱلصَّـٰدِقَـٰتِ وَٱلصَّـٰبِرِينَ وَٱلصَّـٰبِرَٰتِ وَٱلْخَـٰشِعِينَ وَٱلْخَـٰشِعَـٰتِ
وَٱلْمُتَصَدِّقِينَ وَٱلْمُتَصَدِّقَـٰتِ وَٱلصَّـٰٓئِمِينَ وَٱلصَّـٰٓئِمَـٰتِ وَٱلْحَـٰفِظِينَ فُرُوجَهُمْ
وَٱلْحَـٰفِظَـٰتِ وَٱلذَّٰكِرِينَ ٱللَّهَ كَثِيرًا وَٱلذَّٰكِرَٰتِ أَعَدَّ ٱللَّهُ لَهُم مَّغْفِرَةً وَأَجْرًا
عَظِيمًا

Ciertamente, los musulmanes y las musulmanas, los
creyentes y las creyentes, los obedientes y las
obedientes, los veraces y las veraces, los pacientes y las
pacientes, los humildes y las humildes, los caritativos y
las caritativas, los ayunantes y las ayunantes, los
hombres que guardan sus partes privadas y las
mujeres que lo hacen, los hombres que recuerdan a
Allah a menudo y las mujeres que lo hacen, para ellos
Allah ha preparado el perdón y una gran recompensa.

Indeed, the Muslim men and Muslim women, the believing

men and believing women, the obedient men and obedient women, the truthful men and truthful women, the patient men and patient women, the humble men and humble women, the charitable men and charitable women, the fasting men and fasting women, the men who guard their private parts and the women who do so, and the men who remember Allah often and the women who do so - for them Allah has prepared forgiveness and a great reward.

SURAH 35, VERSO 2

مَّا يَفْتَحِ ٱللَّهُ لِلنَّاسِ مِن رَّحْمَةٍ فَلَا مُمْسِكَ لَهَا ۖ وَمَا يُمْسِكْ فَلَا مُرْسِلَ لَهُۥ مِنۢ بَعْدِهِۦ ۚ وَهُوَ ٱلْعَزِيزُ ٱلْحَكِيمُ

Lo que Alá conceda a la gente de misericordia, nadie podrá negárselo; y lo que Él retenga, nadie podrá liberarlo después. Y Él es el Exaltado en Poder, el Sabio.

Whatever Allah grants to people of mercy - none can withhold it; and whatever He withholds - none can release it thereafter. And He is the Exalted in Might, the Wise.

SURAH 42, VERSO 30

وَمَآ أَصَٰبَكُم مِّن مُّصِيبَةٍ فَبِمَا كَسَبَتْ أَيْدِيكُمْ وَيَعْفُواْ عَن كَثِيرٍ

Y lo que os sobrevenga de desastre, es por lo que vuestras manos han ganado; pero Él perdona mucho.

And whatever strikes you of disaster - it is for what your hands have earned; but He pardons much.

SURAH 57, VERSO 22

مَّا أَصَابَ مِن مُّصِيبَةٍ إِلَّا بِإِذْنِ ٱللَّهِ وَمَن يُؤْمِنۢ بِٱللَّهِ يَهْدِ قَلْبَهُۥ وَٱللَّهُ بِكُلِّ شَىْءٍ عَلِيمٌ

No hay catástrofe en la tierra ni entre vosotros que no esté inscrita en un registro antes de que la hagamos realidad.

No disaster strikes upon the earth or among yourselves except that it is in a register before We bring it into being - indeed that, for Allah, is easy.

SURAH 64, VERSO 11

مَّآ أَصَابَ مِن مُّصِيبَةٍ إِلَّا بِإِذْنِ ٱللَّهِ وَمَن يُؤْمِنۢ بِٱللَّهِ يَهْدِ قَلْبَهُۥ وَٱللَّهُ بِكُلِّ
شَىْءٍ عَلِيمٌ

**No hay catástrofe sino con el permiso de Alah. Quien
crea en Alah, Él guiará su corazón. Alah sabe todo.**

*No disaster strikes except by permission of Allah. And
whoever believes in Allah - He will guide his heart. And
Allah is Knowing of all things.*

SURAH 10, VERSO 107

وَإِن يَمْسَسْكَ ٱللَّهُ بِضُرٍّ فَلَا كَاشِفَ لَهُ إِلَّا هُوَ وَإِن يُرِدْكَ بِخَيْرٍ فَلَا رَآدَّ لِفَضْلِهِ يُصِيبُ بِهِ مَن يَشَآءُ مِنْ عِبَادِهِ وَهُوَ ٱلْغَفُورُ ٱلرَّحِيمُ

Y si Alah te toca con la adversidad, no hay quien te la quite salvo Él; y si te quiere hacer el bien, no hay quien repela Su generosidad. Él hace que llegue a quien Él quiere de Sus siervos. Y Él es el Perdonador, el Misericordioso.

And if Allah should touch you with adversity, there is no remover of it except Him; and if He intends for you good, then there is no repeller of His bounty. He causes it to reach whom He wills of His servants. And He is the Forgiving, the Merciful.

Surah 57, Verso 23

لَّقَدْ أَرْسَلْنَا رُسُلَنَا بِٱلْبَيِّنَتِ وَأَنزَلْنَا مَعَهُمُ ٱلْكِتَبَ وَٱلْمِيزَانَ لِيَقُومَ ٱلنَّاسُ
بِٱلْقِسْطِ ۖ وَأَنزَلْنَا ٱلْحَدِيدَ فِيهِ بَأْسٌ شَدِيدٌ وَمَنَفِعُ لِلنَّاسِ وَلِيَعْلَمَ ٱللَّهُ مَن
يَنصُرُهُ وَرُسُلَهُ ۥ بِٱلْغَيْبِ ۚ إِنَّ ٱللَّهَ قَوِىٌّ عَزِيزٌ

**Ya hemos enviado a Nuestros mensajeros con pruebas
claras y hemos hecho descender con ellos la Escritura y
la balanza para que la gente pueda mantener [sus
asuntos] en justicia. Y hemos hecho descender el
hierro, en el que hay gran poder militar y beneficios
para la gente, y para que Alah haga evidentes a
quienes Le apoyan a Él y a Sus mensajeros invisibles.
Alah es Poderoso y Exaltado en Poder.**

*We have already sent Our messengers with clear evidences
and sent down with them the Scripture and the balance that
the people may maintain [their affairs] in justice. And We*

sent down iron, wherein is great military might and benefits
for the people, and so that Allah may make evident those who
support Him and His messengers unseen. Indeed, Allah is
Powerful and Exalted in Might.

SURAH 61, VERSO 11

آمِنُوا بِاللهَّ وَرَسُولِهِ، وَاجْتَهِدُوا فِي سَبِيلِ اللهَّ بِأَمْوَالِكُمْ وَأَنفُسِكُمْ. ذَٰلِكُمْ
خَيْرٌ لَكُمْ إِن كُنتُمْ تَعْلَمُونَ

**Que creáis en Allah y en Su Mensajero, y os esforcéis
en la causa de Allah con vuestros bienes y vuestras
vidas. Esto es mejor para vosotros, si supierais.**

*Believe in Allah and His Messenger, and strive in the cause
of Allah with your wealth and your lives. That is better for
you if you only knew.*

Surah 3, Verso 169

وَلَا تَحْسَبَنَّ ٱلَّذِينَ قُتِلُواْ فِى سَبِيلِ ٱللَّهِ أَمْوَٰتًا بَلْ أَحْيَاءٌ عِندَ رَبِّهِمْ يُرْزَقُونَ

No consideres muertos a los que mueren en el camino de Alá. No, están vivos, con su Señor, y tienen provisión.

Think not of those who are killed in the Way of Allah as dead. Nay, they are alive, with their Lord, and they have provision.

SURAH 22, VERSO 58

وَٱلَّذِينَ هَاجَرُوا۟ فِى سَبِيلِ ٱللَّهِ ثُمَّ قُتِلُوٓا۟ أَوْ مَاتُوا۟ لَيَرْزُقَنَّهُمُ ٱللَّهُ رِزْقًا حَسَنًا وَإِنَّ ٱللَّهَ لَهُوَ خَيْرُ ٱلرَّٰزِقِينَ

Pero a quienes emigraron por la causa de Alá y luego fueron asesinados o murieron, Alá les proporcionará una buena provisión. Y, en verdad, Alá es el mejor de los proveedores.

But those who emigrated for the cause of Allah and then were killed or died - Allah will surely provide for them a good provision. And indeed, it is Allah who is the best of providers.

SURAH 9, VERSO 111

إِنَّ ٱللَّهَ ٱشْتَرَىٰ مِنَ ٱلْمُؤْمِنِينَ أَنفُسَهُمْ وَأَمْوَٰلَهُم بِأَنَّ لَهُمُ ٱلْجَنَّةَ يُقَـٰتِلُونَ فِى
سَبِيلِ ٱللَّهِ فَيَقْتُلُونَ وَيُقْتَلُونَ وَعْدًا عَلَيْهِ حَقًّا فِى ٱلتَّوْرَىٰةِ وَٱلْإِنجِيلِ
وَٱلْقُرْءَانِ وَمَنْ أَوْفَىٰ بِعَهْدِهِۦ مِنَ ٱللَّهِ فَٱسْتَبْشِرُوا۟ بِبَيْعِكُمُ ٱلَّذِى بَايَعْتُم بِهِۦ
وَذَٰلِكَ هُوَ ٱلْفَوْزُ ٱلْعَظِيمُ

**Ciertamente, Alá ha comprado a los creyentes sus
vidas y sus propiedades [a cambio] de que tengan el
Paraíso. Luchan por la causa de Alá, por lo que matan
y son matados. [Es] una promesa verdadera
[vinculante] para Él en la Torá, el Evangelio y el
Corán. ¿Y quién es más fiel a su pacto que Alá?
Alegraos, pues, de la transacción que habéis contraído.
Ése es el gran logro.**

*Indeed, Allah has purchased from the believers their lives
and their properties [in exchange] for that they will have
Paradise. They fight in the cause of Allah, so they kill and*

are killed. [It is] a true promise [binding] upon Him in the Torah and the Gospel and the Qur'an. And who is truer to his covenant than Allah? So rejoice in your transaction which you have contracted. And it is that which is the great attainment.

SURAH 5, VERSO 32

مِنْ أَجْلِ ذَٰلِكَ كَتَبْنَا عَلَىٰ بَنِىٓ إِسْرَٰٓءِيلَ أَنَّهُۥ مَن قَتَلَ نَفْسًۢا بِغَيْرِ نَفْسٍ أَوْ فَسَادٍ فِى ٱلْأَرْضِ فَكَأَنَّمَا قَتَلَ ٱلنَّاسَ جَمِيعًا وَمَنْ أَحْيَاهَا فَكَأَنَّمَآ أَحْيَا ٱلنَّاسَ جَمِيعًا وَلَقَدْ جَآءَتْهُمْ رُسُلُنَا بِٱلْبَيِّنَٰتِ ثُمَّ إِنَّ كَثِيرًا مِّنْهُم بَعْدَ ذَٰلِكَ فِى ٱلْأَرْضِ لَمُسْرِفُونَ

Por eso, decretamos sobre los Hijos de Israel que quien mate a un alma, a menos que sea por un alma o por corrupción [hecha] en la tierra, es como si hubiera matado a toda la humanidad. Y quien salve a uno, es como si hubiera salvado a toda la humanidad. Y nuestros mensajeros vinieron a ellos con pruebas claras. Y, ciertamente, muchos de ellos, [incluso] después de eso, en toda la tierra, fueron transgresores.

Because of that, We decreed upon the Children of Israel that whoever kills a soul unless for a soul or for corruption [done] in the land - it is as if he had slain mankind entirely. And whoever saves one - it is as if he had saved mankind entirely. And our messengers had certainly come to them with clear proofs. Then indeed many of them, [even] after that, throughout the land, were transgressors.

SURAH 60, VERSO 8

ٱللَّهُ لَا يَنْهَىٰكُمْ عَنِ ٱلَّذِينَ لَمْ يُقَٰتِلُوكُمْ فِى ٱلدِّينِ وَلَمْ يُخْرِجُوكُم مِّن دِيَٰرِكُمْ
أَن تَبَرُّوهُمْ وَتُقْسِطُوٓا۟ إِلَيْهِمْ إِنَّ ٱللَّهَ يُحِبُّ ٱلْمُقْسِطِينَ

Alá no os prohíbe -a quienes no os combaten por causa de la religión ni os expulsan de vuestras casas- que seáis rectos con ellos y actuéis con justicia con ellos. Ciertamente, Alá ama a quienes actúan con justicia.

Allah does not forbid you from those who do not fight you because of religion and do not expel you from your homes - from being righteous toward them and acting justly toward them. Indeed, Allah loves those who act justly.

SURAH 6, VERSO 151

قُل تَعَالَوْاْ أَتْلُ مَا حَرَّمَ رَبُّكُمْ عَلَيْكُمْ أَلَّا تُشْرِكُوا۟ بِهِۦ شَيْـًٔا ۖ وَبِٱلْوَٰلِدَيْنِ
إِحْسَٰنًا ۖ وَلَا تَقْتُلُوٓا۟ أَوْلَٰدَكُم مِّنْ إِمْلَٰقٍ ۖ نَّحْنُ نَرْزُقُكُمْ وَإِيَّاهُمْ ۖ وَلَا تَقْرَبُوا۟
ٱلْفَوَٰحِشَ مَا ظَهَرَ مِنْهَا وَمَا بَطَنَ ۖ وَلَا تَقْتُلُوا۟ ٱلنَّفْسَ ٱلَّتِى حَرَّمَ ٱللَّهُ إِلَّا
بِٱلْحَقِّ ۚ ذَٰلِكُمْ وَصَّىٰكُم بِهِۦ لَعَلَّكُمْ تَعْقِلُونَ

**Di: "Venid, os recitaré lo que vuestro Señor os ha
prohibido. [Él os ordena] que no Le asociéis nada, y a
los padres, buen trato, y no matéis a vuestros hijos por
pobreza; Nosotros os proveeremos a vosotros y a ellos.
Y no os acerquéis a las inmoralidades, ni a las que son
aparentes ni a las que son ocultas. Y no matéis el alma
que Alá ha prohibido, salvo por derecho. Esto os ha
instruido para que uséis la razón".**

*Say, "Come, I will recite what your Lord has prohibited to
you. [He commands] that you not associate anything with
Him, and to parents, good treatment, and do not kill your*

children out of poverty; We will provide for you and them. And do not approach immoralities - what is apparent of them and what is concealed. And do not kill the soul which Allah has forbidden, except by right. This has He instructed you that you may use reason."

Surah 24, Verso 22

وَلَا يَأْتَلِ أُوْلُواْ ٱلْفَضْلِ مِنكُمْ وَٱلسَّعَةِ أَن يُؤْتُواْ أُوْلِى ٱلْقُرْبَىٰ وَٱلْمَسَـٰكِينَ
وَٱلْمُهَـٰجِرِينَ فِى سَبِيلِ ٱللَّهِ وَلْيَعْفُواْ وَلْيَصْفَحُوٓاْ أَلَا تُحِبُّونَ أَن يَغْفِرَ ٱللَّهُ
لَكُمْ وَٱللَّهُ غَفُورٌ رَّحِيمُ

**Y que los que entre vosotros sean virtuosos y ricos no
juren no dar [ayuda] a sus parientes y a los necesitados
y a los emigrantes por la causa de Alah, y que
perdonen y pasen por alto. ¿No queréis que Alá os
perdone? Alá es Perdonador y Misericordioso.**

*And let not those of virtue among you and wealth swear not
to give [aid] to their relatives and the needy and the
emigrants for the cause of Allah, and let them pardon and
overlook. Would you not like that Allah should forgive you?
And Allah is Forgiving and Merciful.*

SURAH 17, VERSO 23

وَقَضَىٰ رَبُّكَ أَلَّا تَعْبُدُوٓا۟ إِلَّآ إِيَّاهُ وَبِٱلْوَٰلِدَيْنِ إِحْسَـٰنًا إِمَّا يَبْلُغَنَّ عِندَكَ
ٱلْكِبَرَ أَحَدُهُمَآ أَوْ كِلَاهُمَا فَلَا تَقُل لَّهُمَآ أُفٍّ وَلَا تَنْهَرْهُمَا وَقُل لَّهُمَا قَوْلًا
كَرِيمًا

**Y vuestro Señor ha decretado que no adoréis sino a Él,
y a los padres, buen trato. Si uno de ellos o ambos
llegan a la vejez [mientras] están con vosotros, no les
digáis [ni siquiera]: "uff", y no les rechacéis sino que
habladles con palabras nobles.**

*And your Lord has decreed that you not worship except Him,
and to parents, good treatment. Whether one or both of them
reach old age [while] with you, say not to them [so much as],
"uff," and do not repel them but speak to them a noble word.*

SURAH 17, VERSO 24

وَٱخْفِضْ لَهُمَا جَنَاحَ ٱلذُّلِّ مِنَ ٱلرَّحْمَةِ وَقُل رَّبِّ ٱرْحَمْهُمَا كَمَا رَبَّيَانِى صَغِيرًا

Y bajad hacia ellos el ala de la humildad por piedad y decid: "Señor mío, ten piedad de ellos como ellos me educaron [cuando yo era] pequeño".

And lower to them the wing of humility out of mercy and say, "My Lord, have mercy upon them as they brought me up [when I was] small."

Surah 8, Verso 28

وَٱعْلَمُوٓاْ أَنَّمَآ أَمْوَٰلُكُمْ وَأَوْلَٰدُكُمْ فِتْنَةٌ وَأَنَّ ٱللَّهَ عِندَهُۥٓ أَجْرٌ عَظِيمٌ

Y sabed que vuestras propiedades y vuestros hijos no son sino una prueba y que Alá tiene con Él una gran recompensa.

And know that your properties and your children are but a trial and that Allah has with Him a great reward.

Surah 17, Verso 31

وَلَا تَقْتُلُوٓاْ أَوْلَٰدَكُمْ خَشْيَةَ إِمْلَٰقٍ نَّحْنُ نَرْزُقُهُمْ وَإِيَّاكُمْ إِنَّ قَتْلَهُمْ كَانَ خِطْـًٔا كَبِيرًا

Y no matéis a vuestros hijos por miedo a la pobreza.
Nosotros nos ocupamos de ellos y de vosotros.
Ciertamente, matarlos es siempre un gran pecado.

And do not kill your children for fear of poverty. We provide
for them and for you. Indeed, their killing is ever a great sin.

SURAH 18, VERSO 46

ٱلْمَالُ وَٱلْبَنُونَ زِينَةُ ٱلْحَيَوٰةِ ٱلدُّنْيَا وَٱلْبَٰقِيَٰتُ ٱلصَّٰلِحَٰتُ خَيْرٌ عِندَ رَبِّكَ ثَوَابًا وَخَيْرٌ أَمَلاً

La riqueza y los hijos no son más que adornos de la vida mundana. Pero las buenas acciones duraderas son mejor recompensa para tu Señor y mejor esperanza.

Wealth and children are [but] adornment of the worldly life. But the enduring good deeds are better to your Lord for reward and better for [one's] hope.

SURAH 34, VERSO 37

وَمَا كَانَ لِنَفْسٍ أَن تَمُوتَ إِلَّا بِإِذْنِ ٱللَّهِ كِتَٰبًا مُّؤَجَّلًا وَمَن يُرِدْ ثَوَابَ ٱلدُّنْيَا
نُؤْتِهِۦ مِنْهَا وَمَن يُرِدْ ثَوَابَ ٱلْأَخِرَةِ نُؤْتِهِۦ مِنْهَا وَسَنَجْزِى ٱلشَّٰكِرِينَ

**Nadie puede morir si no es con el permiso de Alah y
en un momento determinado. Y a quien desee la
recompensa de este mundo, se la daremos; y a quien
desee la recompensa de la otra vida, se la daremos. Y
recompensaremos a los agradecidos.**

*And it is not for any soul to die except by permission of Allah
at a decree determined. And whoever desires the reward of
this world - We will give him thereof; and whoever desires the
reward of the Hereafter - We will give him thereof. And we
will reward the grateful.*

SURAH 63, VERSO 9

يَـٰٓأَيُّهَا ٱلَّذِينَ ءَامَنُوا۟ لَا تُلْهِكُمْ أَمْوَٰلُكُمْ وَلَآ أَوْلَـٰدُكُمْ عَن ذِكْرِ ٱللَّهِ وَمَن يَفْعَلْ
ذَٰلِكَ فَأُو۟لَـٰٓئِكَ هُمُ ٱلْخَـٰسِرُونَ

**Oh vosotros que habéis creído, que vuestra riqueza y
vuestros hijos no os aparten del recuerdo de Alá.
Quien lo haga - ése es un perdedor.**

*O you who have believed, let not your wealth and your
children divert you from remembrance of Allah. And
whoever does that - then those are the losers.*

SURAH 43, VERSO 36

وَمَن يُعَظِّمْ شَعَـٰٓئِرَ ٱللَّهِ فَإِنَّهَا مِن تَقْوَى ٱلْقُلُوبِ

**Y quien honre los símbolos de Alá - ciertamente, es
por la piedad de los corazones.**

*And whoever honors the symbols of Allah - indeed, it is from
the piety of hearts.*

SURAH 31, VERSO 7

وَإِذْ قَالَ لُقْمَـٰنُ لِٱبْنِهِۦ وَهُوَ يَعِظُهُۥ يَـٰبُنَىَّ لَا تُشْرِكْ بِٱللَّهِ إِنَّ ٱلشِّرْكَ لَظُلْمٌ
عَظِيمٌ

Y [menciona, Oh Muhammad], cuando Luqman dijo a su hijo mientras le instruía: "Oh hijo mío, no asocies [nada] con Allah. Ciertamente, la asociación [con Él] es una gran injusticia".

And [mention, O Muhammad], when Luqman said to his son while he was instructing him, "O my son, do not associate [anything] with Allah. Indeed, association [with him] is great injustice."

SURAH 20, VERSO 124

وَمَنْ أَعْرَضَ عَن ذِكْرِى فَإِنَّ لَهُۥ مَعِيشَةً ضَنكًا وَنَحْشُرُهُۥ يَوْمَ ٱلْقِيَـٰمَةِ أَعْمَىٰ

Pero quien se aparte de Mi recuerdo, ciertamente tendrá una vida deprimida, y le recogeremos ciego el Día de la Resurrección".

But whoever turns away from My remembrance - indeed, he will have a depressed life, and We will gather him on the Day of Resurrection blind."

SURAH 32, VERSO 22

وَمَن يُسْلِمْ وَجْهَهُ إِلَى ٱللَّهِ وَهُوَ مُحْسِنٌ فَقَدِ ٱسْتَمْسَكَ بِٱلْعُرْوَةِ ٱلْوُثْقَىٰ
وَإِلَى ٱللَّهِ عَاقِبَةُ ٱلْأُمُورِ

**Y quien someta su rostro a Alah mientras hace el bien,
entonces se ha asido al asidero más digno de confianza.
Y a Alah será el resultado de [todos] los asuntos.**

*And whoever submits his face to Allah while he is a doer of
good - then he has grasped the most trustworthy handhold.
And to Allah will be the outcome of [all] matters.*

SURAH 7, VERSO 36

فَٱلَّذِينَ كَذَّبُواْ بِـَٔايَـٰتِنَا وَٱسْتَكْبَرُواْ عَنْهَا لَا تُفَتَّحُ لَهُمْ أَبْوَٰبُ ٱلسَّمَآءِ وَلَا
يَدْخُلُونَ ٱلْجَنَّةَ حَتَّىٰ يَلِجَ ٱلْجَمَلُ فِى سَمِّ ٱلْخِيَاطِ وَكَذَٰلِكَ نَجْزِى ٱلْمُجْرِمِينَ

**Pero quienes niegan Nuestros signos y son arrogantes
con ellos, ésos son los compañeros del Fuego;
permanecerán en él eternamente.**

*But those who deny Our signs and are arrogant toward them
- those are the companions of the Fire; they will abide therein
eternally.*

SURAH 7, VERSO 40

إِنَّ ٱلَّذِينَ كَذَّبُواْ بِـَٔايَـٰتِنَا وَٱسْتَكْبَرُواْ عَنْهَا لَا تُفَتَّحُ لَهُمْ أَبْوَٰبُ ٱلسَّمَاءِ وَلَا
يَدْخُلُونَ ٱلْجَنَّةَ حَتَّىٰ يَلِجَ ٱلْجَمَلُ فِى سَمِّ ٱلْخِيَاطِ وَكَذَٰلِكَ نَجْزِى ٱلْمُجْرِمِينَ

**A quienes nieguen Nuestros signos y sean arrogantes
con ellos no se les abrirán las puertas del Cielo ni
entrarán en el Paraíso hasta que un camello entre por
el ojo de una aguja. Así recompensamos a los
criminales.**

*Indeed, those who deny Our verses and are arrogant toward
them - the gates of Heaven will not be opened for them, nor
will they enter Paradise until a camel enters into the eye of a
needle. And thus do We recompense the criminals.*

SURAH 3, VERSO 135

وَٱلَّذِينَ إِذَا فَعَلُوا۟ فَٰحِشَةً أَوْ ظَلَمُوٓا۟ أَنفُسَهُمْ ذَكَرُوا۟ ٱللَّهَ فَٱسْتَغْفَرُوا۟ لِذُنُوبِهِمْ وَمَن يَغْفِرُ ٱلذُّنُوبَ إِلَّا ٱللَّهُ وَلَمْ يُصِرُّوا۟ عَلَىٰ مَا فَعَلُوا۟ وَهُمْ يَعْلَمُونَ

Y quienes, cuando cometen una inmoralidad o se equivocan [por transgresión], se acuerdan de Alá y buscan el perdón de sus pecados -¿y quién puede perdonar los pecados sino Alá? - y no persisten en lo que han hecho mientras lo saben.

And those who, when they commit an immorality or wrong themselves [by transgression], remember Allah and seek forgiveness for their sins - and who can forgive sins except Allah? - and [who] do not persist in what they have done while they know.

SURAH 53, VERSO 32

وَمَا هُوَ عَلَى ٱلْغَيْبِ بِضَنِينٍ

Y que no retenga [el conocimiento de] lo oculto.

And he is not a withholder of [knowledge of] the unseen.

SURAH 4, VERSO 31

إِن تَجْتَنِبُواْ كَبَائِرَ مَا تُنْهَوْنَ عَنْهُ نُكَفِّرْ عَنكُمْ سَيِّئَاتِكُمْ وَنُدْخِلْكُم مُّدْخَلاً
كَرِيمًا

**Si evitáis los pecados mayores que os están prohibidos,
os quitaremos los pecados menores y os admitiremos a
una entrada noble [en el Paraíso].**

*If you avoid the major sins which you are forbidden, We will
remove from you your lesser sins and admit you to a noble
entrance [into Paradise].*

SURAH 3, VERSO 90

إِنَّ ٱلَّذِينَ كَفَرُواْ بَعْدَ إِيمَـٰنِهِمْ ثُمَّ ٱزْدَادُواْ كُفْرًا لَّن تُقْبَلَ تَوْبَتُهُمْ وَأُوْلَـٰئِكَ هُمُ ٱلضَّآلُّونَ

Ciertamente, a quienes no creen después de haber creído y luego aumentan su incredulidad, nunca se les aceptará su [pretendido] arrepentimiento, y ellos son los extraviados.

Indeed, those who disbelieve after their belief and then increase in disbelief - never will their [claimed] repentance be accepted, and they are the ones astray.

Surah 4, Verso 137

إِنَّ ٱلَّذِينَ ءَامَنُواْ ثُمَّ كَفَرُواْ ثُمَّ ءَامَنُواْ ثُمَّ كَفَرُواْ ثُمَّ ٱزْدَادُواْ كُفْرًا لَّن يَكُنِ ٱللَّهُ لِيَغْفِرَ لَهُمْ وَلَا لِيَهْدِيَهُمْ سَبِيلًا

Ciertamente, a los que han creído y después han descreído, después han creído, después han descreído y después han aumentado su incredulidad, Alá no les perdonará jamás ni les guiará por un camino.

Indeed, those who have believed then disbelieved, then believed, then disbelieved, and then increased in disbelief - never will Allah forgive them, nor will He guide them to a way.

SURAH 4, VERSO 18

وَلَا تَكُونُواْ كَٱلَّذِينَ نَسُواْ ٱللَّهَ فَأَنسَىٰهُمْ أَنفُسَهُمْ أُوْلَـٰٓئِكَ هُمُ ٱلْفَـٰسِقُونَ

Y no seáis como los que olvidaron a Alá y Él les hizo olvidarse de sí mismos. Ésos son los desobedientes desafiantes.

And do not be like those who forgot Allah, so He made them forget themselves. Those are the defiantly disobedient.

SURAH 2, VERSO 81

بَلَىٰ مَن كَسَبَ سَيِّئَةً وَأَحَاطَتْ بِهِۦ خَطِيٓئَتُهُۥ فَأُو۟لَٰٓئِكَ أَصْحَٰبُ ٱلنَّارِ هُمْ فِيهَا خَٰلِدُونَ

Sí, pero quien se gane el mal y su pecado le haya envuelto, ésos son los compañeros del Fuego; permanecerán en él eternamente.

Yes, but whoever earns evil and his sin has encompassed him - those are the companions of the Fire; they will abide therein eternally.

SURAH 39, VERSO 65

وَقَدْ نُزِّلَ عَلَيْكَ فِى ٱلْكِتَبِ أَنْ إِذَا سَمِعْتُمْ ءَايَتِ ٱللَّهِ يُكْفَرُ بِهَا وَيُسْتَهْزَأُ
بِهَا فَلَا تَقْعُدُوا۟ مَعَهُمْ حَتَّىٰ يَخُوضُوا۟ فِى حَدِيثٍ غَيْرِهِۦٓ إِنَّكُمْ إِذًا مِّثْلُهُمْ إِنَّ
ٱللَّهَ جَامِعُ ٱلْمُنَفِقِينَ وَٱلْكَفِرِينَ فِى جَهَنَّمَ جَمِيعًا

**Y ya se os ha revelado en el Libro [este Corán] que
cuando oís [recitar] los versículos de Alá, son negados
[por ellos] y ridiculizados; así que no os sentéis con
ellos hasta que entablen otra conversación. Entonces
seréis como ellos. Alah reunirá en el Infierno a los
hipócritas y a los incrédulos.**

*And it has already been revealed to you in the Book [this
Quran] that when you hear the verses of Allah [recited], they
are denied [by them] and ridiculed; so do not sit with them
until they enter into another conversation. Indeed, you would
then be like them. Indeed Allah will gather the hypocrites
and disbelievers in Hell all together.*

Surah 5, Verso 90

يَـٰٓأَيُّهَا ٱلَّذِينَ ءَامَنُوٓا۟ إِنَّمَا ٱلْخَمْرُ وَٱلْمَيْسِرُ وَٱلْأَنصَابُ وَٱلْأَزْلَـٰمُ رِجْسٌ مِّنْ
عَمَلِ ٱلشَّيْطَـٰنِ فَٱجْتَنِبُوهُ لَعَلَّكُمْ تُفْلِحُونَ

Oh creyentes, ciertamente, las bebidas embriagantes, el juego, los altares de piedra y las flechas de adivinación no son más que impurezas de la obra de Satanás, así que evitadlas para que tengáis éxito.

O you who have believed, indeed, intoxicants, gambling, [sacrificing on] stone alters [to other than Allah], and divining arrows are but defilement from the work of Satan, so avoid it that you may be successful.

SURAH 17, VERSO 32

وَلَا تَقْرَبُواْ ٱلزِّنَىٰٓ إِنَّهُۥ كَانَ فَٰحِشَةً وَسَآءَ سَبِيلاً

Y no te acerques a las relaciones sexuales ilícitas. En verdad, siempre es una inmoralidad y es malo como camino.

And do not approach unlawful sexual intercourse. Indeed, it is ever an immorality and is evil as a way.

Surah 24, Verso 2

ٱلزَّانِى لَا يَنكِحُ إِلَّا زَانِيَةً أَوْ مُشْرِكَةً وَٱلزَّانِيَةُ لَا يَنكِحُهَا إِلَّا زَانٍ أَوْ مُشْرِكٌ
وَحُرِّمَ ذَٰلِكَ عَلَى ٱلْمُؤْمِنِينَ

A la mujer [soltera] o al hombre [soltero] hallados culpables de mantener relaciones sexuales, azotadlos con cien latigazos a cada uno, y no os compadezcáis de ellos en la religión de Alah, si creéis en Alah y en el Último Día. Y que un grupo de creyentes presencie su castigo.

The [unmarried] woman or [unmarried] man found guilty of sexual intercourse - lash each one of them with a hundred lashes, and do not be taken by pity for them in the religion of Allah, if you should believe in Allah and the Last Day. And let a group of the believers witness their punishment.

Surah 24, Verso 19

إِنَّ ٱلَّذِينَ يُحِبُّونَ أَن تَشِيعَ ٱلْفَٰحِشَةُ فِى ٱلَّذِينَ ءَامَنُواْ لَهُمْ عَذَابٌ أَلِيمٌ فِى ٱلدُّنْيَا وَٱلْءَاخِرَةِ وَٱللَّهُ يَعْلَمُ وَأَنتُمْ لَا تَعْلَمُونَ

Ciertamente, quienes quieran que se difunda [o publicite] la inmoralidad entre los que han creído tendrán un castigo doloroso en este mundo y en el Más Allá. Y Alá sabe y vosotros no sabéis.

Indeed, those who like that immorality should be spread [or publicized] among those who have believed will have a painful punishment in this world and the Hereafter. And Allah knows and you do not know.

SURAH 5, VERSO 38

السَّارِقُ وَالسَّارِقَةُ فَاقْطَعُوا أَيْدِيَهُمَا جَزَاءً بِمَا كَسَبَا نَكَالًا مِّنَ اللَّهِ ۗ وَاللَّهُ عَزِيزٌ حَكِيمٌ

[Para] el ladrón, al hombre y a la mujer, amputadles las manos en recompensa por lo que cometieron como [castigo] disuasorio de Alá. Y Alá es Exaltado en Poder y Sabio.

[As for] the thief, the male and the female, amputate their hands in recompense for what they committed as a deterrent [punishment] from Allah. And Allah is Exalted in Might and Wise.

SURAH 2, VERSO 276

يَمْحَقُ اللَّهُ الرِّبَا وَيُرْبِي الصَّدَقَاتِ ۗ وَاللَّهُ لَا يُحِبُّ كُلَّ كَفَّارٍ أَثِيمٍ

Alah destruye los intereses y aumenta las caridades. A Alah no le agrada todo incrédulo que peca.

Allah destroys interest and gives increase for charities. And Allah does not like every sinning disbeliever.

SURAH 11, VERSO 52

يَا قَوْمِ اسْتَغْفِرُوا رَبَّكُمْ ثُمَّ تُوبُوا إِلَيْهِ يُرْسِلِ السَّمَاءَ عَلَيْكُم مِّدْرَارًا وَيَزِدْكُمْ
قُوَّةً إِلَى قُوَّتِكُمْ وَلَا تَتَوَلَّوْا مُجْرِمِينَ

**Dijo [Noé]: "Oh pueblo mío, pedid perdón a vuestro
Señor y luego arrepentíos ante Él. Él enviará [lluvia
del] cielo sobre vosotros en lluvias y os aumentará en
fuerza [añadida] a vuestra fuerza. Y no os apartéis,
[siendo] delincuentes".**

[Noah] said, "O my people, ask forgiveness of your Lord
and then repent to Him. He will send [rain from] the sky
upon you in showers and increase you in strength [added]
to your strength. And do not turn away, [being] criminals."

SURAH 4, VERSO 49

أَلَمْ تَرَ إِلَى الَّذِينَ يُزَكُّونَ أَنفُسَهُم بَلِ اللَّهُ يُزَكِّي مَن يَشَاءُ وَلَا يُظْلَمُونَ
فَتِيلًا

**¿Acaso no has visto a los que dicen ser puros? Más
bien, Alá purifica a quien quiere y no se comete
injusticia con ellos, [ni siquiera] tanto como un hilo
[dentro de una semilla de dátil].**

*Have you not seen those who claim themselves to be pure?
Rather, Allah purifies whom He wills, and injustice is not
done to them, [even] as much as a thread [inside a date
seed].*

Surah 6, Verso 159

إِنَّ الَّذِينَ فَرَّقُوا دِينَهُمْ وَكَانُوا شِيَعًا لَّسْتَ مِنْهُمْ فِي شَيْءٍ ۚ إِنَّمَا أَمْرُهُمْ
إِلَى اللَّهِ ثُمَّ يُنَبِّئُهُم بِمَا كَانُوا يَفْعَلُونَ

**Ciertamente, los que han dividido su religión y se han
convertido en sectas, tú, [Oh Muhammad], no estás
[asociado] con ellos en nada. Su asunto sólo [queda] en
manos de Alá; entonces Él les informará de lo que
solían hacer.**

*Indeed, those who have divided their religion and become
sects - you, [O Muhammad], are not [associated] with them
in anything. Their affair is only [left] to Allah; then He will
inform them about what they used to do.*

SURAH 22, VERSO 78

وَجَاهِدُوا فِي اللَّهِ حَقَّ جِهَادِهِ ۚ هُوَ اجْتَبَاكُمْ وَمَا جَعَلَ عَلَيْكُمْ فِي الدِّينِ مِنْ حَرَجٍ ۚ مِّلَّةَ أَبِيكُمْ إِبْرَاهِيمَ ۚ هُوَ سَمَّاكُمُ الْمُسْلِمِينَ مِن قَبْلُ وَفِي هَـٰذَا لِيَكُونَ الرَّسُولُ شَهِيدًا عَلَيْكُمْ وَتَكُونُوا شُهَدَاءَ عَلَى النَّاسِ ۚ فَأَقِيمُوا الصَّلَاةَ وَآتُوا الزَّكَاةَ وَاعْتَصِمُوا بِاللَّهِ هُوَ مَوْلَاكُمْ ۖ فَنِعْمَ الْمَوْلَىٰ وَنِعْمَ النَّصِيرُ

Y lucha por Alá con el esfuerzo que Le es debido. Él os ha elegido y no os ha puesto ninguna dificultad en la religión. [Es la religión de vuestro padre, Abraham. Alá os nombró "musulmanes" antes [en escrituras anteriores] y en ésta [revelación] para que el Mensajero sea testigo sobre vosotros y vosotros seáis testigos sobre la gente. Estableced la oración, dad el zakat y aferraos a Alá. Él es vuestro Protector, y excelente es el protector y excelente es el auxiliador.

And strive for Allah with the striving due to Him. He has chosen you and has not placed upon you in the religion any difficulty. [It is] the religion of your father, Abraham. Allah named you "Muslims" before [in former scriptures] and in this [revelation] that the Messenger may be a witness over you and you may be witnesses over the people. So establish prayer and give zakah and hold fast to Allah. He is your protector; and excellent is the protector, and excellent is the helper.

SURAH 42, VERSO 13

شَرَعَ لَكُم مِّنَ الدِّينِ مَا وَصَّىٰ بِهِ نُوحًا وَالَّذِي أَوْحَيْنَا إِلَيْكَ وَمَا وَصَّيْنَا بِهِ إِبْرَاهِيمَ وَمُوسَىٰ وَعِيسَىٰ ۖ أَنْ أَقِيمُوا الدِّينَ وَلَا تَتَفَرَّقُوا فِيهِ ۚ كَبُرَ عَلَى الْمُشْرِكِينَ مَا تَدْعُوهُمْ إِلَيْهِ ۚ اللَّهُ يَجْتَبِي إِلَيْهِ مَن يَشَاءُ وَيَهْدِي إِلَيْهِ مَن يُنِيبُ

Os ha ordenado de religión lo que ordenó a Noé y lo que te hemos revelado a ti, [Oh Muhammad], y lo que ordenamos a Abraham y a Moisés y a Jesús: establecer la religión y no estar divididos en ella. Difícil para quienes asocian a otros con Alá es aquello a lo que les invitáis. Alah escoge para Sí a quien quiere y guía hacia Sí a quien se vuelve [a Él].

He has ordained for you of religion what He enjoined upon Noah and that which We have revealed to you, [O Muhammad], and what We enjoined upon Abraham and Moses and Jesus - to establish the religion and not be divided therein. Difficult for those who associate others with Allah is that to which you invite them. Allah chooses for Himself whom He wills and guides to Himself whoever turns back [to Him].

SURAH 33, VERSO 40

مَّا كَانَ مُحَمَّدٌ أَبَا أَحَدٍ مِّن رِّجَالِكُمْ وَلَـٰكِن رَّسُولَ اللَّهِ وَخَاتَمَ النَّبِيِّينَ ۗ وَكَانَ
اللَّهُ بِكُلِّ شَيْءٍ عَلِيمًا

**Muhammad no es el padre de ninguno de vosotros,
sino el Enviado de Alá y el último de los profetas. Y
Alá es Conocedor de todas las cosas.**

*Muhammad is not the father of [any] one of your men, but
[he is] the Messenger of Allah and last of the prophets. And
ever is Allah, of all things, Knowing.*

Surah 49, Verso 2

يَا أَيُّهَا الَّذِينَ آمَنُوا لَا تَرْفَعُوا أَصْوَاتَكُمْ فَوْقَ صَوْتِ النَّبِيِّ وَلَا تَجْهَرُوا لَهُ
بِالْقَوْلِ كَجَهْرِ بَعْضِكُمْ لِبَعْضٍ أَن تَحْبَطَ أَعْمَالُكُمْ وَأَنتُمْ لَا تَشْعُرُونَ

**Oh, vosotros que habéis creído, no elevéis la voz por
encima de la del Profeta ni le habléis tan alto como
algunos de vosotros a otros, no sea que vuestras obras
pierdan valor sin que os deis cuenta.**

*O you who have believed, do not raise your voices above the
voice of the Prophet or be loud to him in speech like the
loudness of some of you to others, lest your deeds become
worthless while you perceive not.*

SURAH 2, VERSO 285

آمَنَ الرَّسُولُ بِمَا أُنزِلَ إِلَيْهِ مِن رَّبِّهِ وَالْمُؤْمِنُونَ ۚ كُلٌّ آمَنَ بِاللَّهِ وَمَلَائِكَتِهِ وَكُتُبِهِ وَرُسُلِهِ لَا نُفَرِّقُ بَيْنَ أَحَدٍ مِّن رُّسُلِهِ ۚ وَقَالُوا سَمِعْنَا وَأَطَعْنَا ۖ غُفْرَانَكَ رَبَّنَا وَإِلَيْكَ الْمَصِيرُ

El Mensajero ha creído en lo que le fue revelado de su Señor, y [también] los creyentes. Todos ellos han creído en Alá y en Sus ángeles y en Sus libros y en Sus mensajeros, [diciendo]: "No hacemos distinción entre ninguno de Sus mensajeros". Y dicen: "Oímos y obedecemos. [Buscamos] Tu perdón, Señor nuestro, y a Ti es el destino [final]".

The Messenger has believed in what was revealed to him from his Lord, and [so have] the believers. All of them have believed in Allah and His angels and His books and His messengers, [saying], "We make no distinction between any of His messengers." And they say, "We hear and we obey. [We seek] Your forgiveness, our Lord, and to You is the [final] destination."

SURAH 37, VERSO 181

إِلَّا عِبَادَ اللَّهِ الْمُخْلَصِينَ

Excepto los siervos elegidos de Alá [que son] sinceros [en la fe].

Except for the chosen servants of Allah [who are] sincere [in faith].

SURAH 10, VERSO 62

أَلَا إِنَّ أَوْلِيَاءَ اللَّهِ لَا خَوْفٌ عَلَيْهِمْ وَلَا هُمْ يَحْزَنُونَ

**Sin duda, [para] los aliados de Alá no existirá temor
en cuanto a ellos, ni tampoco se afligirán.**

*Unquestionably, [for] the allies of Allah there will be no fear
concerning them, nor will they grieve.*

SURAH 2, VERSO 255

اللّهُ لَا إِلَهَ إِلَّا هُوَ الْحَيُّ الْقَيُّومُ ۚ لَا تَأْخُذُهُ سِنَةٌ وَلَا نَوْمٌ ۚ لَّهُ مَا فِي
السَّمَاوَاتِ وَمَا فِي الْأَرْضِ ۗ مَن ذَا الَّذِي يَشْفَعُ عِندَهُ إِلَّا بِإِذْنِهِ ۚ يَعْلَمُ مَا
بَيْنَ أَيْدِيهِمْ وَمَا خَلْفَهُمْ ۖ وَلَا يُحِيطُونَ بِشَيْءٍ مِّنْ عِلْمِهِ إِلَّا بِمَا شَاءَ ۚ وَسِعَ
كُرْسِيُّهُ السَّمَاوَاتِ وَالْأَرْضَ ۖ وَلَا يَئُودُهُ حِفْظُهُمَا ۚ وَهُوَ الْعَلِيُّ الْعَظِيمُ

**Allah - no hay deidad salvo Él, el Viviente, el
Sustentador de [toda] la existencia. Ni la somnolencia
ni el sueño Le alcanzan. A Él pertenece cuanto hay en
los cielos y cuanto hay en la tierra. ¿Quién puede
interceder ante Él si no es con Su permiso? Él conoce
lo que está [actualmente] ante ellos y lo que estará
después de ellos, y no abarcan nada de Su
conocimiento salvo lo que Él quiere. Su Kursi se
extiende por los cielos y la tierra, y su conservación no
Le cansa. Él es el Altísimo, el Más Grande.**

Allah - there is no deity except Him, the Ever-Living, the

Sustainer of [all] existence. Neither drowsiness overtakes Him nor sleep. To Him belongs whatever is in the heavens and whatever is on the earth. Who is it that can intercede with Him except by His permission? He knows what is [presently] before them and what will be after them, and they encompass not a thing of His knowledge except for what He wills. His Kursi extends over the heavens and the earth, and their preservation tires Him not. And He is the Most High, the Most Great.

SURAH 3, VERSO 26

قُلِ اللَّهُمَّ مَالِكَ الْمُلْكِ تُؤْتِي الْمُلْكَ مَن تَشَاءُ وَتَنزِعُ الْمُلْكَ مِمَّن تَشَاءُ وَتُعِزُّ مَن تَشَاءُ وَتُذِلُّ مَن تَشَاءُ ۖ بِيَدِكَ الْخَيْرُ ۖ إِنَّكَ عَلَىٰ كُلِّ شَيْءٍ قَدِيرٌ

Di: "Oh Alá, Dueño de la Soberanía, Tú das la soberanía a quien Tú quieres y quitas la soberanía a quien Tú quieres. Tú honras a quien quieres y humillas a quien quieres. En Tu mano está el bien. En verdad, Tú eres competente sobre todas las cosas.

Say, "O Allah, Owner of Sovereignty, You give sovereignty to whom You will and You take sovereignty away from whom You will. You honor whom You will and You humble whom You will. In Your hand is [all] good. Indeed, You are over all things competent.

SURAH 28, VERSO 56

إِنَّكَ لَا تَهْدِي مَنْ أَحْبَبْتَ وَلَٰكِنَّ اللَّهَ يَهْدِي مَن يَشَاءُ ۚ وَهُوَ أَعْلَمُ بِالْمُهْتَدِينَ

En verdad, [Oh Muhammad], tú no guías a quien quieres, sino que Allah guía a quien Él quiere. Y Él es el más sabio de los guiados.

Indeed, [O Muhammad], you do not guide whom you like, but Allah guides whom He wills. And He is most knowing of the [rightly] guided.

SURAH 3, VERSO 129

وَلِلَّهِ مَا فِي السَّمَاوَاتِ وَمَا فِي الْأَرْضِ ۚ يَعْفُو عَن مَّن يَشَاءُ وَيُعَذِّبُ مَن يَشَاءُ ۚ وَاللَّهُ غَفُورٌ رَّحِيمٌ

A Alá pertenece cuanto hay en los cielos y cuanto hay en la tierra. Él perdona a quien quiere y castiga a quien quiere. Alah es Perdonador y Misericordioso.

To Allah belongs whatever is in the heavens and whatever is in the earth. He forgives whom He wills and punishes whom He wills. And Allah is Forgiving and Merciful.

SURAH 28, VERSO 88

وَلَا تَدْعُ مَعَ اللهِ إِلَـٰهًا آخَرَ ۘ لَا إِلَـٰهَ إِلَّا هُوَ ۚ كُلُّ شَيْءٍ هَالِكٌ إِلَّا وَجْهَهُ ۚ لَهُ الْحُكْمُ وَإِلَيْهِ تُرْجَعُونَ

Y no invoquéis con Alá a otra divinidad. No hay más deidad que Él. Todo será destruido salvo Su Rostro. Suyo es el juicio y a Él seréis devueltos.

And do not invoke with Allah another deity. There is no deity except Him. Everything will be destroyed except His Face. His is the judgement, and to Him you will be returned.

SURAH 40, VERSO 65

هُوَ الْحَيُّ لَا إِلَهَ إِلَّا هُوَ فَادْعُوهُ مُخْلِصِينَ لَهُ الدِّينَ ۗ الْحَمْدُ للَّهِ رَبِّ الْعَالَمِينَ

Él es el Eterno; no hay deidad salvo Él, así que invócale, [siéndole] sincero en la religión. [Todas las alabanzas son para Alá, Señor de los mundos.

He is the Ever-Living; there is no deity except Him, so call upon Him, [being] sincere to Him in religion. [All] praise is [due] to Allah, Lord of the worlds.

SURAH 72, VERSO 20

قُلْ إِنَّمَا أَدْعُو رَبِّي وَلَا أُشْرِكُ بِهِ أَحَدًا

Di: "Sólo invoco a mi Señor y no Le asocio a nadie".

Say, "I only invoke my Lord and do not associate with Him anyone."

Surah 72, Verso 21

قُلْ إِنِّي لَا أَمْلِكُ لَكُمْ ضَرًّا وَلَا رَشَدًا

**Di: "Ciertamente, no poseo para ti [el poder del] mal
ni la recta dirección".**

*Say, "Indeed, I do not possess for you [the power of] harm or
right direction."*

SURAH 72, VERSO 22

قُلْ إِنِّي لَن يُجِيرَنِي مِنَ اللَّهِ أَحَدٌ وَلَنْ أَجِدَ مِن دُونِهِ مُلْتَحَدًا

Di: "En verdad, nunca me protegerá de Alá nadie [si desobedezco], ni encontraré en otro que no sea Él un refugio".

Say, "Indeed, there will never protect me from Allah anyone [if I should disobey], nor will I find in other than Him a refuge.

SURAH 47, VERSO 19

فَاعْلَمْ أَنَّهُ لَا إِلَـهَ إِلَّا اللهُ وَاسْتَغْفِرْ لِذَنبِكَ وَلِلْمُؤْمِنِينَ وَالْمُؤْمِنَاتِ ۗ وَاللهُ يَعْلَمُ
مُتَقَلَّبَكُمْ وَمَثْوَاكُمْ

**Sabe, pues, [Oh Muhammad], que no hay más deidad
que Allah y pide perdón por tu pecado y por los
hombres y mujeres creyentes. Y Alá conoce tus
movimientos y tu lugar de descanso.**

*So know, [O Muhammad], that there is no deity except
Allah and ask forgiveness for your sin and for the believing
men and believing women. And Allah knows of your
movement and your resting place.*

SURAH 2, VERSO 286

لَا يُكَلِّفُ اللَّهُ نَفْسًا إِلَّا وُسْعَهَا ۚ لَهَا مَا كَسَبَتْ وَعَلَيْهَا مَا اكْتَسَبَتْ ۗ رَبَّنَا لَا
تُؤَاخِذْنَا إِن نَّسِينَا أَوْ أَخْطَأْنَا ۚ رَبَّنَا وَلَا تَحْمِلْ عَلَيْنَا إِصْرًا كَمَا حَمَلْتَهُ
عَلَى الَّذِينَ مِن قَبْلِنَا ۚ رَبَّنَا وَلَا تُحَمِّلْنَا مَا لَا طَاقَةَ لَنَا بِهِ ۖ وَاعْفُ عَنَّا وَاغْفِرْ
لَنَا وَارْحَمْنَا ۚ أَنتَ مَوْلَانَا فَانصُرْنَا عَلَى الْقَوْمِ الْكَافِرِينَ

**Alá no carga al alma más allá de lo que puede soportar.
Tendrá [la consecuencia de] lo [bueno] que haya
ganado, y soportará [la consecuencia de] lo [malo] que
haya ganado. "Señor nuestro, no nos culpes si hemos
olvidado o errado. Señor nuestro, no nos impongas
una carga como la que Tú impusiste a los que nos
precedieron. Señor nuestro, y no nos cargues con lo
que no somos capaces de soportar. Y perdónanos, y
ten piedad de nosotros. Tú eres nuestro protector, así
que danos la victoria sobre la gente incrédula".**

Allah does not burden a soul beyond that it can bear. It will have [the consequence of] what [good] it has gained, and it will bear [the consequence of] what [evil] it has earned. "Our Lord, do not impose blame upon us if we have forgotten or erred. Our Lord, and lay not upon us a burden like that which You laid upon those before us. Our Lord, and burden us not with that which we have no ability to bear. And pardon us; and forgive us; and have mercy upon us. You are our protector, so give us victory over the disbelieving people."

SURAH 16, VERSO 32

الَّذِينَ تَتَوَفَّاهُمُ الْمَلَائِكَةُ طَيِّبِينَ ۙ يَقُولُونَ سَلَامٌ عَلَيْكُمُ ادْخُلُوا الْجَنَّةَ بِمَا
كُنتُمْ تَعْمَلُونَ

**Aquellos a que los ángeles acojan en la muerte [siendo]
buenos y puros - [los ángeles] dirán: "La paz sea
contigo. Entrad en el Paraíso por lo que hacíais".**

*Those whom the angels take in death [while] good and pure -
[the angels] will say, "Peace be upon you. Enter Paradise for
what you used to do."*

SURAH 15, VERSO 99

وَعْبُدْ رَبَّكَ حَتَّىٰ يَأْتِيَكَ الْيَقِينُ

Y adorad a vuestro Señor hasta que os llegue la certeza (de la muerte).

And worship your Lord until there comes to you the certainty (death).

Referencias De Las Oraciones:

SURAH 26, VERSO 83

رَبِّ هَبْ لِي حُكْمًا وَأَلْحِقْنِي بِالصَّالِحِينَ

"Señor mío, concédeme autoridad y júntame con los justos".

"My Lord, grant me authority and join me with the righteous."

SURAH 3, VERSO 36

رَبِّ إِنِّي وَهَنَ الْعَظْمُ مِنِّي وَاشْتَعَلَ الرَّأْسُ شَيْبًا وَلَمْ أَكُن بِدُعَائِكَ رَبِّ شَقِيًّا

"Mi Señor, ciertamente mis huesos se han debilitado, y mi cabeza se ha llenado de blanco, y nunca he sido infeliz en mi súplica a Ti, mi Señor".

"My Lord, indeed my bones have weakened, and my head has filled with white, and never have I been in my supplication to You, my Lord, unhappy."

SURAH 37, VERSO 100

رَبِّ ارْجِعُونِ * لَعَلِّي عَمِلُ صَالِحًا فِيمَا تَرَكْتُ كَلًّا إِنَّهَا كَلِمَةٌ هُوَ قَائِلُهَا
وَمِن وَرَائِهِم بَرْزَخٌ إِلَى يَوْمِ يُبْعَثُونَ

**"Señor mío, devuélveme [a la vida] * para que haga justicia en lo que dejé". ¡No! Es sólo una palabra lo que dice; y detrás de ellas hay una barrera hasta el Día en que resuciten.
"Señor mío, no me dejes solo [sin heredero], siendo Tú el mejor de los herederos".**

"My Lord, return me [to life] * so that I may do righteousness in that which I left." No! It is only a word he is saying; and behind them is a barrier until the Day they are resurrected.

SURAH 21, VERSO 89

رَبِّ لَا تَذَرْنِي فَرْدًا وَأَنتَ خَيْرُ الْوَارِثِينَ

"Señor mío, concédeme de Ti una buena descendencia. En verdad, Tú eres el Oyente de la súplica".

"My Lord, do not leave me alone [with no heir], while you are the best of inheritors."

SURAH 3, VERSO 38

رَبِّ هَبْ لِي مِن لَّدُنكَ ذُرِّيَّةً طَيِّبَةً إِنَّكَ سَمِيعُ الدُّعَاءِ

**"Señor mío, concédeme de Ti una buena descendencia.
En verdad, Tú eres el Oyente de la súplica".**

*"My Lord, grant me from Yourself a good offspring. Indeed,
You are the Hearer of supplication."*

SURAH 38, VERSO 35

رَبِّ هَبْ لِي مِنَ الصَّالِحِينَ

"Señor mío, concédeme [un hijo] de entre los justos".

"My Lord, grant me [a child] from among the righteous."

Surah 23, Verso 109

رَبِّ فَلَا تُخْزِنِي يَوْمَ يُبْعَثُونَ

"Señor mío, no me deshonres el Día en que resuciten".

*"My Lord, do not disgrace me on the Day they are
resurrected."*

SURAH 23, VERSO 118

رَبِّ اغْفِرْ وَارْحَمْ وَأَنتَ خَيْرُ الرَّاحِمِينَ

"Señor mío, perdona y ten piedad, Tú eres el mejor de los misericordiosos".

"My Lord, forgive and have mercy, and You are the best of the merciful."

SURAH 21, VERSO 83

رَبِّ لَا تَذَرْنِي فَرْدًا وَأَنتَ خَيْرُ الْوَارِثِينَ

**"Señor mío, no me dejes solo [sin heredero], siendo Tú
el mejor de los herederos".**

*"My Lord, do not leave me alone [with no heir], while you
are the best of inheritors."*

SURAH 21, VERSO 87

رَبَّنَا لَا تَجْعَلْنَا فِتْنَةً لِّلَّذِينَ كَفَرُوا وَاغْفِرْ لَنَا رَبَّنَا ۚ إِنَّكَ أَنتَ الْعَزِيزُ الْحَكِيمُ

"Señor nuestro, no nos conviertas en prueba para la gente malhechora. Y perdónanos, Señor nuestro. En verdad, Tú eres el Exaltado en Poder, el Sabio".

"Our Lord, do not make us a trial for the wrongdoing people. And forgive us, our Lord. Indeed, You are the Exalted in Might, the Wise."

SURAH 14, VERSO 40

رَبِّ اجْعَلْنِي مُقِيمَ الصَّلَاةِ وَمِن ذُرِّيَّتِي ۚ رَبَّنَا وَتَقَبَّلْ دُعَاءِ

"Señor nuestro, haz de mí un instaurador de la oración, y [de muchos] de mis descendientes. Señor nuestro, y acepta mi súplica".

"My Lord, make me an establisher of prayer, and [many] from my descendants. Our Lord, and accept my supplication."

SURAH 14, VERSO 41

رَبَّنَا اغْفِرْ لِي وَلِوَالِدَيَّ وَلِلْمُؤْمِنِينَ يَوْمَ يَقُومُ الْحِسَابُ

"Señor nuestro, perdóname a mí, a mis padres y a los creyentes el Día en que se establezca la cuenta".

"Our Lord, forgive me and my parents and the believers the Day the account is established."

SURAH 71, VERSO 28

رَّبِّ اغْفِرْ لِي وَلِوَالِدَيَّ وَلِمَن دَخَلَ بَيْتِيَ مُؤْمِنًا وَلِلْمُؤْمِنِينَ وَالْمُؤْمِنَاتِ وَلَا تَزِدِ الظَّالِمِينَ إِلَّا تَبَارًا

"Señor mío, perdóname a mí y a mis padres y a quien entre en mi casa creyente y a los hombres y mujeres creyentes. Y no aumentes los malhechores sino en destrucción".

"My Lord, forgive me and my parents and whoever enters my house a believer and the believing men and believing women. And do not increase the wrongdoers except in destruction."

SURAH 4, VERSO 86

وَإِذَا حُيِّيتُم بِتَحِيَّةٍ فَحَيُّوا بِأَحْسَنَ مِنْهَا أَوْ رُدُّوهَا ۗ إِنَّ اللَّهَ كَانَ عَلَىٰ كُلِّ شَيْءٍ حَسِيبًا

"Y cuando te saluden con un saludo, saluda [a cambio] con uno mejor que él o [al menos] devuélvelo [de igual manera]. Ciertamente, Alá es siempre, sobre todas las cosas, un Contable".

"And when you are greeted with a greeting, greet [in return] with one better than it or [at least] return it [in a like manner]. Indeed, Allah is ever, over all things, an Accountant."

SURAH 12, VERSO 101

يَا صَاحِبَيِ السِّجْنِ أَأَرْبَابٌ مُّتَفَرِّقُونَ خَيْرٌ أَمِ اللَّهُ الْوَاحِدُ الْقَهَّارُ

"Oh, mis dos compañeros de prisión, ¿son mejores los señores separados o Alá, el Único, el Prevalente?"

O my two companions of prison, are separate lords better or Allah, the One, the Prevailing?

Referencias de los 20 mejores versículos del Sagrado Corán para cristianos

SURAH 3, VERSO 42

وَإِذْ قَالَتِ الْمَلَائِكَةُ يَا مَرْيَمُ إِنَّ اللَّهَ اصْطَفَاكِ وَطَهَّرَكِ وَاصْطَفَاكِ عَلَى نِسَاءِ الْعَالَمِينَ

Y [recuerda] cuando los ángeles dijeron: "¡Oh, María! Ciertamente, Allah te ha escogido, te ha purificado y te ha escogido sobre todas las mujeres de los mundos."

And [mention] when the angels said, "O Mary, indeed Allah has chosen you and purified you and chosen you above the women of the worlds.

SURAH, 3 VERSO 45

إِذْ قَالَتِ الْمَلَائِكَةُ يَا مَرْيَمُ إِنَّ اللَّهَ يُبَشِّرُكِ بِكَلِمَةٍ مِنْهُ اسْمُهُ الْمَسِيحُ عِيسَى ابْنُ مَرْيَمَ وَجِيهًا فِي الدُّنْيَا وَالْآخِرَةِ وَمِنَ الْمُقَرَّبِينَ

[Recuerda] cuando los ángeles dijeron: "¡Oh, María! Allah te anuncia la buena nueva de una palabra de Él, cuyo nombre será el Mesías, Jesús, hijo de María, distinguido en este mundo y en el otro y será de los allegados [a Allah]."

[And mention] when the angels said, "O Mary, Allah gives you good tidings of a word from Him, whose name will be the Messiah, Jesus, the son of Mary - distinguished in this world and the Hereafter and among those brought near [to Allah].

SURAH 3, VERSO 47

قَالَتْ رَبِّ أَنَّى يَكُونُ لِي وَلَدٌ وَلَمْ يَمْسَسْنِي بَشَرٌ قَالَ كَذَٰلِكِ اللَّهُ يَخْلُقُ مَا يَشَاءُ ۚ إِذَا قَضَىٰ أَمْرًا فَإِنَّمَا يَقُولُ لَهُ كُن فَيَكُونُ

Ella dijo: "¡Señor! ¿Cómo podré tener un hijo si ningún hombre me ha tocado?" [El ángel] dijo: "Así será. Allah crea lo que Él quiere. Cuando decreta algo, simplemente dice: '¡Sé!' y es."

She said, "My Lord, how will I have a child when no man has touched me?" [The angel] said, "Such is Allah; He creates what He wills. When He decrees a matter, He only says to it, 'Be,' and it is."

SURAH 3, VERSO 59

إِنَّ مَثَلَ عِيسَى عِندَ اللَّهِ كَمَثَلِ آدَمَ خَلَقَهُ مِنْ تُرَابٍ ثُمَّ قَالَ لَهُ كُن فَيَكُونُ

**La semejanza de Jesús ante Allah es como la de Adán.
Él lo creó de tierra y luego dijo: "¡Sé!" y fue.**

*Indeed, the example of Jesus to Allah is like that of Adam.
He created Him from dust; then He said to him, "Be," and
he was.*

SURAH 19, VERSO 35

مَا كَانَ لِلَّهِ أَنْ يَتَّخِذَ مِنْ وَلَدٍ ۖ سُبْحَانَهُ ۚ إِذَا قَضَىٰ أَمْرًا فَإِنَّمَا يَقُولُ لَهُ كُنْ فَيَكُونُ

No conviene a Allah tomar ningún hijo. ¡Glorificado sea! Cuando decreta algo, solo dice: "¡Sé!" y es.

It is not [befitting] for Allah to take a son; exalted is He! When He decrees an affair, He only says to it, "Be," and it is.

Surah 66, Verso 12

وَمَرْيَمَ ابْنَتَ عِمْرَانَ الَّتِي أَحْصَنَتْ فَرْجَهَا فَنَفَخْنَا فِيهِ مِنْ رُوحِنَا وَصَدَّقَتْ
بِكَلِمَاتِ رَبِّهَا وَكُتُبِهِ وَكَانَتْ مِنَ الْقَانِتِينَ

**Y a María, hija de 'Imran, que guardó su castidad;
insuflamos en ella de Nuestro espíritu y creyó en las
palabras de su Señor y en Sus libros, y fue de los
devotos.**

*And [the example of] Mary, the daughter of 'Imran, who
guarded her chastity, so We blew into [her garment] through
Our angel, and she believed in the words of her Lord and His
scriptures and was of the devoutly obedient.*

SURAH 5, VERSO 17

إِنَّ الَّذِينَ قَالُوا إِنَّ اللَّهَ هُوَ الْمَسِيحُ ابْنُ مَرْيَمَ قَدْ كَفَرُوا ۚ قُلْ فَمَن يَمْلِكُ مِنَ اللَّهِ شَيْئًا إِنْ أَرَادَ أَن يُهْلِكَ الْمَسِيحَ ابْنَ مَرْيَمَ وَأُمَّهُ وَمَن فِي الْأَرْضِ جَمِيعًا ۗ وَلِلَّهِ مُلْكُ السَّمَاوَاتِ وَالْأَرْضِ وَمَا بَيْنَهُمَا ۚ يَخْلُقُ مَا يَشَاءُ ۚ وَاللَّهُ عَلَىٰ كُلِّ شَيْءٍ قَدِيرٌ

Han descreído quienes dicen: "Allah es el Mesías, hijo de María." Di: "¿Y quién podría impedir a Allah si Él quisiera destruir al Mesías, hijo de María, a su madre y a todos los que hay en la Tierra? A Allah pertenece el dominio de los cielos y la Tierra y todo lo que hay entre ellos. Él crea lo que quiere. Allah es Omnipotente."

Indeed, those who say, "Allah is the Messiah, son of Mary," have disbelieved. Say, "Who could prevent Allah if He willed to destroy the Messiah, son of Mary, or his mother, or everyone on earth? And to Allah belongs the dominion of the heavens and the earth and whatever is between them. He creates what He wills, and Allah is over all things competent."

Surah 4, Verso 171

يَا أَهْلَ الْكِتَابِ لَا تَغْلُوا فِي دِينِكُمْ وَلَا تَقُولُوا عَلَى اللَّهِ إِلَّا الْحَقَّ إِنَّمَا الْمَسِيحُ عِيسَى ابْنُ مَرْيَمَ رَسُولُ اللَّهِ وَكَلِمَتُهُ أَلْقَاهَا إِلَى مَرْيَمَ وَرُوحٌ مِّنْهُ فَآمِنُوا بِاللَّهِ وَرُسُلِهِ وَلَا تَقُولُوا ثَلَاثَةٌ انتَهُوا خَيْرًا لَّكُمْ إِنَّمَا اللَّهُ إِلَٰهٌ وَاحِدٌ سُبْحَانَهُ أَن يَكُونَ لَهُ وَلَدٌ لَّهُ مَا فِي السَّمَاوَاتِ وَمَا فِي الْأَرْضِ وَكَفَىٰ بِاللَّهِ وَكِيلًا

O gente del Libro, no exageréis en vuestra religión y no digáis de Allah sino la verdad. El Mesías, Jesús, hijo de María, es solo un Mensajero de Allah, Su palabra que Él dirigió a María y un espíritu [procedente] de Él. Creed, pues, en Allah y en Sus mensajeros y no digáis "tres". Desistid, es mejor para vosotros. Allah es solo un Dios único. ¡Glorificado sea de tener un hijo! Suyo es cuanto hay en los cielos y en la Tierra y Allah es suficiente como Protector.

O People of the Scripture, do not commit excess in your

171

religion or say about Allah except the truth. The Messiah, Jesus, the son of Mary, was but a messenger of Allah and His word which He directed to Mary and a soul [created at a command] from Him. So believe in Allah and His messengers. And do not say, "Three"; desist - it is better for you. Indeed, Allah is but one God. Exalted is He above having a son. To Him belongs whatever is in the heavens and whatever is on the earth. And sufficient is Allah as Disposer of affairs.

SURAH 5, VERSO 72

لَّقَدْ كَفَرَ الَّذِينَ قَالُوا إِنَّ اللَّهَ هُوَ الْمَسِيحُ ابْنُ مَرْيَمَ ۖ وَقَالَ الْمَسِيحُ يَا بَنِي إِسْرَائِيلَ اعْبُدُوا اللَّهَ رَبِّي وَرَبَّكُمْ ۖ إِنَّهُ مَن يُشْرِكْ بِاللَّهِ فَقَدْ حَرَّمَ اللَّهُ عَلَيْهِ الْجَنَّةَ وَمَأْوَاهُ النَّارُ ۖ وَمَا لِلظَّالِمِينَ مِنْ أَنصَارٍ

Han descreído quienes dicen: "Allah es el Mesías, hijo de María", siendo así que el Mesías dijo: "¡Oh, hijos de Israel! Adorad a Allah, mi Señor y vuestro Señor. Quien asocie algo a Allah, a ese Allah le prohibirá el Paraíso, y su refugio será el Fuego. Y para los opresores no habrá quien les auxilie."

They have certainly disbelieved who say, "Allah is the Messiah, son of Mary." But the Messiah said, "O Children of Israel, worship Allah, my Lord and your Lord." Indeed, he who associates others with Allah - Allah has forbidden him Paradise, and his refuge is the Fire. And there are not for the wrongdoers any helpers.

SURAH 5, VERSO 73

لَّقَدْ كَفَرَ الَّذِينَ قَالُوا إِنَّ اللَّهَ ثَالِثُ ثَلَاثَةٍ ۘ وَمَا مِنْ إِلَٰهٍ إِلَّا إِلَٰهٌ وَاحِدٌ ۚ وَإِن لَّمْ
يَنتَهُوا عَمَّا يَقُولُونَ لَيَمَسَّنَّ الَّذِينَ كَفَرُوا مِنْهُمْ عَذَابٌ أَلِيمٌ

**Han descreído quienes dicen: "Allah es uno de tres."
No hay más dios que un Dios único. Si no desisten de
lo que dicen, un castigo doloroso alcanzará a quienes
de ellos hayan descreído.**

*They have certainly disbelieved who say, "Allah is one of
three in a Trinity." But there is no god except one God. If they
do not desist from what they are saying, a painful
punishment will surely afflict the disbelievers among them.*

SURAH 5, VERSO 75

مَّا الْمَسِيحُ ابْنُ مَرْيَمَ إِلَّا رَسُولٌ قَدْ خَلَتْ مِن قَبْلِهِ الرُّسُلُ وَأُمُّهُ صِدِّيقَةٌ ۖ
كَانَا يَأْكُلَانِ الطَّعَامَ ۗ انظُرْ كَيْفَ نُبَيِّنُ لَهُمُ الْآيَاتِ ثُمَّ انظُرْ أَنَّىٰ يُؤْفَكُونَ

El Mesías, hijo de María, no fue más que un mensajero. Antes de él pasaron otros mensajeros. Y su madre era una veraz. Ambos comían alimentos. Observa cómo les aclaramos los signos, luego observa cómo se desvían.

The Messiah, son of Mary, was not but a messenger; [other] messengers had passed on before him. And his mother was a supporter of truth. They both used to eat food. Look how We make clear to them the signs; then look how they are deluded.

Surah 5, Verso 116

وَإِذْ قَالَ اللَّهُ يَا عِيسَى ابْنَ مَرْيَمَ أَأَنتَ قُلْتَ لِلنَّاسِ اتَّخِذُونِي وَأُمِّيَ إِلَٰهَيْنِ
مِن دُونِ اللَّهِ ۖ قَالَ سُبْحَانَكَ مَا يَكُونُ لِي أَنْ أَقُولَ مَا لَيْسَ لِي بِحَقٍّ ۚ إِن
كُنتُ قُلْتُهُ فَقَدْ عَلِمْتَهُ ۚ تَعْلَمُ مَا فِي نَفْسِي وَلَا أَعْلَمُ مَا فِي نَفْسِكَ ۚ إِنَّكَ أَنتَ
عَلَّامُ الْغُيُوبِ

Y Al-lah dirá (a Jesús el Día de la Resurrección):
"¿Dijiste tú a los hombres: "Tomadme a mí y a mi
madre por dos dioses aparte de Al-lah"?' Él dirá:
'¡Gloria a Ti! No me corresponde decir lo que no
tengo derecho [a decir]. Si lo hubiese dicho, Tú lo
habrías sabido. Tú sabes lo que hay en mi corazón,
aunque yo no sé lo que hay en el Tuyo. Ciertamente,
Tú eres el Conocedor de todos los secretos."

And [beware the Day] when Allah will say, "O Jesus, Son of
Mary, did you say to the people, 'Take me and my mother as

deities besides Allah?" He will say, "Exalted are You! It was not for me to say that to which I have no right. If I had said it, You would have known it. You know what is within me, and I do not know what is within You. It is You who are Knower of the hidden."

SURAH 5, VERSO 117

وَإِذْ قَالَ اللَّهُ يَا عِيسَى ابْنَ مَرْيَمَ أَأَنتَ قُلْتَ لِلنَّاسِ اتَّخِذُونِي وَأُمِّيَ إِلَٰهَيْنِ
مِن دُونِ اللَّهِ ۖ قَالَ سُبْحَانَكَ مَا يَكُونُ لِي أَنْ أَقُولَ مَا لَيْسَ لِي بِحَقٍّ ۚ إِن
كُنتُ قُلْتُهُ فَقَدْ عَلِمْتَهُ ۚ تَعْلَمُ مَا فِي نَفْسِي وَلَا أَعْلَمُ مَا فِي نَفْسِكَ ۚ إِنَّكَ أَنتَ
عَلَّامُ الْغُيُوبِ

**"No les dije sino lo que Tú me ordenaste: '¡Servid a
Dios, mi Señor y vuestro Señor!' Y fui testigo de ellos
mientras estuve entre ellos, pero cuando me hiciste
morir, Tú fuiste el vigilante sobre ellos. Tú eres testigo
de todas las cosas."**

*I only told them what You commanded me: 'Worship Allah
– my Lord and your Lord.' And I was a witness over them,
as long as I was among them. But when You took me, You
were the Watcher over them – You are Witness over all
things.*

SURAH 5, VERSO 118

مَا قُلْتُ لَهُمْ إِلَّا مَا أَمَرْتَنِي بِهِ أَنِ اعْبُدُوا اللَّهَ رَبِّي وَرَبَّكُمْ ۚ وَكُنتُ عَلَيْهِمْ
شَهِيدًا مَّا دُمْتُ فِيهِمْ ۖ فَلَمَّا تَوَفَّيْتَنِي كُنتَ أَنتَ الرَّقِيبَ عَلَيْهِمْ ۚ وَأَنتَ عَلَىٰ
كُلِّ شَيْءٍ شَهِيدٌ

**Si los castigas, son Tus siervos; y si los perdonas, Tú
eres el Poderoso, el Sabio.**

*If You punish them, they are Your servants; but if You forgive
them: it is you who are the Mighty and Wise.*

SURAH 5, VERSO 110

إِذْ قَالَ اللَّهُ يَا عِيسَى ابْنَ مَرْيَمَ اذْكُرْ نِعْمَتِي عَلَيْكَ وَعَلَىٰ وَالِدَتِكَ إِذْ أَيَّدْتُكَ
بِرُوحِ الْقُدُسِ تُكَلِّمُ النَّاسَ فِي الْمَهْدِ وَكَهْلًا ۖ وَإِذْ عَلَّمْتُكَ الْكِتَابَ وَالْحِكْمَةَ
وَالتَّوْرَاةَ وَالْإِنجِيلَ ۖ وَإِذْ تَخْلُقُ مِنَ الطِّينِ كَهَيْئَةِ الطَّيْرِ بِإِذْنِي فَتَنفُخُ فِيهَا
فَتَكُونُ طَيْرًا بِإِذْنِي ۖ وَتُبْرِئُ الْأَكْمَهَ وَالْأَبْرَصَ بِإِذْنِي ۖ وَإِذْ تُخْرِجُ الْمَوْتَىٰ
بِإِذْنِي ۖ وَإِذْ كَفَفْتُ بَنِي إِسْرَائِيلَ عَنكَ إِذْ جِئْتَهُم بِالْبَيِّنَاتِ فَقَالَ الَّذِينَ
كَفَرُوا مِنْهُمْ إِنْ هَٰذَا إِلَّا سِحْرٌ مُبِينٌ

**Cuando Alá dirá: '¡Jesús, hijo de María! Recuerda Mi
favor hacia ti y hacia tu madre cuando te fortalecí con
el Espíritu Santo para que hablaras a la gente en la
cuna y de adulto. Y cuando te enseñé la Escritura, la
sabiduría, la Tora y el Evangelio. Y cuando creabas de
arcilla algo semejante a un pájaro, con Mi permiso,
soplándole luego para que se convirtiera en un pájaro,
con Mi permiso. Y curabas al ciego de nacimiento y al
leproso, con Mi permiso. Y cuando sacabas a los
muertos, con Mi permiso. Y cuando aparté de ti a los**

Hijos de Israel cuando viniste a ellos con las pruebas claras y los que no creían entre ellos dijeron: 'Esto no es más que manifiesta magia.'

Then Allah will say, "O Jesus, son of Mary, remember My favor upon you and upon your mother when I supported you with the Holy Spirit and you spoke to the people in the cradle and in maturity; and [remember] when I taught you writing and wisdom and the Torah and the Gospel; and when you designed from clay [what was] like the form of a bird with My permission, then you breathed into it, and it became a bird with My permission; and you healed the blind and the leper with My permission; and when you brought forth the dead with My permission; and when I restrained the Children of Israel from [killing] you when you came to them with clear proofs and those who disbelieved among them said, "This is not but obvious magic."

SURAH 4, VERSO 157

وَقَوْلِهِمْ إِنَّا قَتَلْنَا الْمَسِيحَ عِيسَى ابْنَ مَرْيَمَ رَسُولَ اللَّهِ وَمَا قَتَلُوهُ وَمَا
صَلَبُوهُ وَلَٰكِن شُبِّهَ لَهُمْ وَإِنَّ الَّذِينَ اخْتَلَفُوا فِيهِ لَفِي شَكٍّ مِّنْهُ مَا لَهُم بِهِ
مِنْ عِلْمٍ إِلَّا اتِّبَاعَ الظَّنِّ وَمَا قَتَلُوهُ يَقِينًا

Y [también] por su dicho: "Ciertamente, hemos matado al Mesías, Jesús, hijo de María, el Mensajero de Allah." Pero no lo mataron ni lo crucificaron, sino que les pareció así. Y quienes discrepan sobre ello están en duda. No tienen conocimiento cierto, sino que siguen conjeturas. Pero ciertamente, no lo mataron.

And for their saying, "We have killed the Messiah, Jesus, the son of Mary, the Messenger of Allah." In fact, they did not kill him, nor did they crucify him, but it appeared to them as if they did. Those who differ over it are in doubt about it. They have no knowledge of it except the following of assumption. And they did not kill him, for certain.

Surah 4, Verso 158

بَل رَّفَعَهُ اللهُ إِلَيْهِ ۚ وَكَانَ اللهُ عَزِيزًا حَكِيمًا

Más bien, Allah lo elevó hacia Sí. Y Allah es Poderoso, Sabio.

But Allah raised himupon Himself. Allah is Might and Wise.

SURAH 4, VERSO 159

وَإِن مِّنْ أَهْلِ الْكِتَابِ إِلَّا لَيُؤْمِنَّ بِهِ قَبْلَ مَوْتِهِ ۖ وَيَوْمَ الْقِيَامَةِ يَكُونُ عَلَيْهِمْ شَهِيدًا

No hay nadie de la gente del Libro que no creerá en él antes de su muerte. Y el Día de la Resurrección, él será testigo contra ellos.

And there is none from the People of the Scripture but that he will surely believe in Jesus before his death. And on the Day of Resurrection he will be a witness against them.

SURAH 3, VERSO 55

إِذْ قَالَ اللَّهُ يَا عِيسَى إِنِّي مُتَوَفِّيكَ وَرَافِعُكَ إِلَيَّ وَمُطَهِّرُكَ مِنَ الَّذِينَ كَفَرُوا وَجَاعِلُ الَّذِينَ اتَّبَعُوكَ فَوْقَ الَّذِينَ كَفَرُوا إِلَىٰ يَوْمِ الْقِيَامَةِ ۖ ثُمَّ إِلَيَّ مَرْجِعُكُمْ فَأَحْكُمُ بَيْنَكُمْ فِيمَا كُنتُمْ فِيهِ تَخْتَلِفُونَ

[Recuerda] cuando Allah dijo: "¡Oh, Jesús! Voy a poner fin a tu vida terrenal y elevarte a Mí, y librarte de los que no creen y hacer que quienes te siguen superen a quienes no creen hasta el Día de la Resurrección. Luego, a Mí será vuestro retorno y juzgaré entre vosotros sobre aquello en lo que solíais diferir."

Allah said, "O Jesus, indeed I will take you and raise you to Myself and purify you from those who disbelieve and make those who follow you [in submission to Allah alone] superior to those who disbelieve until the Day of Resurrection. Then to

Me is your return, and I will judge between you regarding your disputes."

Surah 5, Verso 82

لَتَجِدَنَّ أَشَدَّ النَّاسِ عَدَاوَةً لِلَّذِينَ آمَنُوا الْيَهُودَ وَالَّذِينَ أَشْرَكُوا ۖ وَلَتَجِدَنَّ أَقْرَبَهُم مَّوَدَّةً لِّلَّذِينَ آمَنُوا الَّذِينَ قَالُوا إِنَّا نَصَارَىٰ ۚ ذَٰلِكَ بِأَنَّ مِنْهُمْ قِسِّيسِينَ وَرُهْبَانًا وَأَنَّهُمْ لَا يَسْتَكْبِرُونَ

Encontrarás que los más intensos en enemistad contra los creyentes son los judíos y los que asocian otros dioses con Allah; y encontrarás que los más cercanos en afecto a los creyentes son quienes dicen: "Somos cristianos." Esto es así porque entre ellos hay sacerdotes y monjes y no son arrogantes.

You will surely find the most intense of the people in animosity toward the believers [to be] the Jews and those who associate others with Allah, and you will find the nearest of them in affection to the believers those who say, "We are Christians." That is because among them are priests and monks and because they are not arrogant.

Referencias de los Párrafos:

SURAH 112

قُلْ هُوَ اللَّهُ أَحَدٌ ١ اللَّهُ الصَّمَدُ ٢ لَمْ يَلِدْ وَلَمْ يُولَدْ ٣ وَلَمْ يَكُن لَّهُ كُفُوًا أَحَدٌ ٤

Di: Él es Allah, Uno, Allah, el Eterno Refugio. No engendra, ni ha sido engendrado, Y no hay nada ni nadie que se le pueda comparar.

Say, "He is Allah, [who is] One, Allah, the Eternal Refuge. He neither begets nor is born, Nor is there to Him any equivalent."

SURAH 1

بِسْمِ اللَّهِ الرَّحْمَنِ الرَّحِيمِ
الْحَمْدُ لِلَّهِ رَبِّ الْعَالَمِينَ
الرَّحْمَنِ الرَّحِيمِ
مَالِكِ يَوْمِ الدِّينِ
إِيَّاكَ نَعْبُدُ وَإِيَّاكَ نَسْتَعِينُ
اهْدِنَا الصِّرَاطَ الْمُسْتَقِيمَ
صِرَاطَ الَّذِينَ أَنْعَمْتَ عَلَيْهِمْ غَيْرِ الْمَغْضُوبِ عَلَيْهِمْ وَلَا الضَّالِّينَ

¡En el nombre de Ala, el Compasivo, el
Misericordioso!
¡Alabado sea Ala, Senor del universe,
el Compasivo, el Misericordioso!
¡Dueno del dia del Juicio,
A Ti solo servimos ya Ti solo imploramos ayuda!
¡Dirigenos por la via recta,
la via de los que Tu has agraciado, no de los que han
incurrido en la ira, ni de los extraviados!

In the name of Allah, the Most Gracious, the Most Merciful.

Praise be to Allah, the Lord of all the worlds.
The Most Gracious, the Most Merciful.
Master of the Day of Judgment.
You alone we worship, and You alone we ask for help.
Guide us on the Straight Path,
the path of those who have received Your grace; not the path of
those who have brought down wrath upon themselves, nor of
those who go astray.

SURAH 57, VERSOS 1, 2 Y 3

سَبَّحَ لِلَّهِ مَا فِي السَّمَاوَاتِ وَالْأَرْضِ ۖ وَهُوَ الْعَزِيزُ الْحَكِيمُ
لَهُ مُلْكُ السَّمَاوَاتِ وَالْأَرْضِ ۖ يُحْيِي وَيُمِيتُ ۖ وَهُوَ عَلَىٰ كُلِّ شَيْءٍ قَدِيرٌ
هُوَ الْأَوَّلُ وَالْآخِرُ وَالظَّاهِرُ وَالْبَاطِنُ ۖ وَهُوَ بِكُلِّ شَيْءٍ عَلِيمٌ

**Todo cuanto hay en los cielos y en la tierra glorifica a
Allah; Él es el Poderoso, el Sabio.
Suyo es el dominio de los cielos y la tierra. Da la vida y
la muerte, y es poderoso sobre todas las cosas.
Él es el Primero y el Último, el Manifiesto y el Oculto,
y es Omnisciente.**

*Whatever is in the heavens and earth exalts Allah, and He is
the Mighty, the Wise.
His is the dominion of the heavens and earth. He gives life
and causes death, and He is over all things competent.
He is the First and the Last, the Ascendant and the Intimate,
and He is, of all things, Knowing.*

SURAH 59, VERSOS 22, 23 Y 24

هُوَ اللَّهُ الَّذِي لَا إِلَهَ إِلَّا هُوَ عَالِمُ الْغَيْبِ وَالشَّهَادَةِ هُوَ الرَّحْمَنُ الرَّحِيمُ
هُوَ اللَّهُ الَّذِي لَا إِلَهَ إِلَّا هُوَ الْمَلِكُ الْقُدُّوسُ السَّلَامُ الْمُؤْمِنُ الْمُهَيْمِنُ الْعَزِيزُ
الْجَبَّارُ الْمُتَكَبِّرُ سُبْحَانَ اللَّهِ عَمَّا يُشْرِكُونَ
هُوَ اللَّهُ الْخَالِقُ الْبَارِئُ الْمُصَوِّرُ لَهُ الْأَسْمَاءُ الْحُسْنَىٰ يُسَبِّحُ لَهُ مَا فِي
السَّمَاوَاتِ وَالْأَرْضِ وَهُوَ الْعَزِيزُ الْحَكِيمُ

Él es Allah, no hay divinidad excepto Él, el Conocedor de lo oculto y lo manifiesto. Él es el Compasivo, el Misericordioso.

Él es Allah, no hay divinidad excepto Él, el Rey, el Santísimo, la Paz, el Dador de Seguridad, el Vigilante, el Todopoderoso, el Fuerte, el Soberbio. ¡Glorificado sea Allah por encima de lo que Le asocian!

Él es Allah, el Creador, el Originador, el Formador. A Él pertenecen los Nombres más hermosos. Todo cuanto está en los cielos y la tierra Le glorifica. Y Él es el Todopoderoso, el Sabio.

He is Allah, other than whom there is no deity, Knower of the unseen and the witnessed. He is the Entirely Merciful, the Especially Merciful.

He is Allah, other than whom there is no deity, the Sovereign, the Pure, the Perfection, the Bestower of Faith, the Overseer, the Exalted in Might, the Compeller, the Superior. Exalted is Allah above whatever they associate with Him.

He is Allah, the Creator, the Inventor, the Fashioner; to Him belong the best names. Whatever is in the heavens and earth is exalting Him. And He is the Exalted in Might, the Wise.

SURAH 97

إِنَّا أَنزَلْنَاهُ فِي لَيْلَةِ الْقَدْرِ

وَمَا أَدْرَاكَ مَا لَيْلَةُ الْقَدْرِ

لَيْلَةُ الْقَدْرِ خَيْرٌ مِّنْ أَلْفِ شَهْرٍ

تَنَزَّلُ الْمَلَائِكَةُ وَالرُّوحُ فِيهَا بِإِذْنِ رَبِّهِم مِّن كُلِّ أَمْرٍ

سَلَامٌ هِيَ حَتَّىٰ مَطْلَعِ الْفَجْرِ

En verdad, lo revelamos en la Noche del Destino.
¿Y cómo te harás una idea de lo que es la Noche del
Destino?
La Noche del Destino es mejor que mil meses.
En ella descienden los ángeles y el Espíritu por
permiso de su Señor con todos los decretos.
Esa noche es [de] paz hasta el amanecer.

Indeed, We sent it [the Qur'an] down during the Night of
Decree.

And what can make you know what is the Night of Decree?
The Night of Decree is better than a thousand months.
The angels and the Spirit descend therein by permission of
their Lord for every matter.
Peace it is until the emergence of dawn.

SURAH 31, VERSOS 17, 18, Y 19

يَا بُنَيَّ أَقِمِ الصَّلَاةَ وَأْمُرْ بِالْمَعْرُوفِ وَانْهَ عَنِ الْمُنكَرِ وَاصْبِرْ عَلَى مَا أَصَابَكَ إِنَّ ذَلِكَ مِنْ عَزْمِ الْأُمُورِ
وَلَا تُصَعِّرْ خَدَّكَ لِلنَّاسِ وَلَا تَمْشِ فِي الْأَرْضِ مَرَحًا إِنَّ اللهَ لَا يُحِبُّ كُلَّ مُخْتَالٍ فَخُورٍ
وَاقْصِدْ فِي مَشْيِكَ وَاغْضُضْ مِنْ صَوْتِكَ إِنَّ أَنكَرَ الْأَصْوَاتِ لَصَوْتُ الْحَمِيرِ

"¡Oh, hijo mío! Mantén la oración, ordena lo que está
bien, prohíbe lo que está mal y ten paciencia ante lo
que te suceda. Eso es, ciertamente, de lo más firme que
se puede hacer.

No desvíes despectivamente tu mejilla hacia la gente,
ni camines por la tierra con insolencia. Ciertamente,
Allah no ama a cada uno que es arrogante y
jactancioso.

Y sé moderado en tu paso y baja tu voz, pues

ciertamente, los sonidos más desagradables son los bramidos de los asnos."

"O my son, establish prayer, enjoin what is right, forbid what is wrong, and be patient over what befalls you. Indeed, that is of the matters [requiring] determination.
And do not turn your cheek [in contempt] toward people and do not walk through the earth exultantly. Indeed, Allah does not like everyone self-deluded and boastful.
And be moderate in your pace and lower your voice; indeed, the most disagreeable of sounds is the voice of donkeys."

Surah 6, Versos 161, 162 y 163

قُلْ إِنَّنِي هَدَانِي رَبِّي إِلَىٰ صِرَاطٍ مُسْتَقِيمٍ دِينًا قِيَمًا مِلَّةَ إِبْرَاهِيمَ حَنِيفًا
وَمَا كَانَ مِنَ الْمُشْرِكِينَ
قُلْ إِنَّ صَلَاتِي وَنُسُكِي وَمَحْيَايَ وَمَمَاتِي لِلَّهِ رَبِّ الْعَالَمِينَ
لَا شَرِيكَ لَهُ ۖ وَبِذَٰلِكَ أُمِرْتُ وَأَنَا أَوَّلُ الْمُسْلِمِينَ

Di: "Ciertamente, mi Señor me ha guiado a un camino recto, una religión correcta, la milicia de Abraham, el monoteísta, y él no fue de los politeístas."
Di: "Ciertamente, mi oración, mi rito, mi vida y mi muerte son para Allah, el Señor de los mundos."
No tiene asociado. Esto me ha sido ordenado, y yo soy el primero de los musulmanes.

Say, "Indeed, my Lord has guided me to a Straight Path, a correct religion, the way of Abraham, inclining toward truth. And he was not among those who associated others with Allah."

Say, "Indeed, my prayer, my rites of sacrifice, my living and
my dying are for Allah, Lord of the worlds."
No partner has He. And this I have been commanded, and I
am the first [among you] of the Muslims.

SURAH 26, VERSOS 78, 79, 80, 81 Y 82

الَّذِي خَلَقَنِي فَهُوَ يَهْدِينِ
وَالَّذِي هُوَ يُطْعِمُنِي وَيَسْقِينِ
وَإِذَا مَرِضْتُ فَهُوَ يَشْفِينِ
وَالَّذِي يُمِيتُنِي ثُمَّ يُحْيِينِ
وَالَّذِي أَطْمَعُ أَن يَغْفِرَ لِي خَطِيئَتِي يَوْمَ الدِّينِ

"El que me creó y me guía,
el que me alimenta y me da de beber,
y cuando enfermo, me sana,
el que me hará morir y luego me dará vida,
y el que espero que me perdone mis faltas el Día del
Juicio."

"He who created me, and He guides me;
He who feeds me and gives me drink;
And when I am ill, it is He who cures me;

He who will cause me to die and then bring me to life;
And who, I hope, will forgive me my faults on the Day of
Judgment."

SURAH 26, VERSOS 87, 88, 89, 90 Y 91

وَلَا تُخْزِنِي يَوْمَ يُبْعَثُونَ
يَوْمَ لَا يَنفَعُ مَالٌ وَلَا بَنُونَ
إِلَّا مَنْ أَتَى اللَّهَ بِقَلْبٍ سَلِيمٍ
وَأُزْلِفَتِ الْجَنَّةُ لِلْمُتَّقِينَ
وَبُرِّزَتِ الْجَحِيمُ لِلْغَاوِينَ

**"Y no me humilles el día que sean resucitados,
el día en que ni la riqueza ni los hijos servirán de
nada,
salvo quien se presente ante Allah con un corazón
sano.
Y se acercará el Paraíso a los piadosos,
mientras que el Infierno se hará visible para los
extraviados."**

"And do not disgrace me on the day they are [all] resurrected

The Day when neither wealth nor sons will avail,
Except for one who comes to Allah with a sound heart.
And Paradise will be brought near [that Day] to the
righteous,
and Hellfire will be brought forth for the deviators."

Surah 72, Versos 20, 21, 22 y 23

قُل إِنَّمَا أَدْعُو رَبِّي وَلَا أُشْرِكُ بِهِ أَحَدًا
وَأَن لَّوِ اسْتَقَمُوا عَلَى الطَّرِيقَةِ لَأَسْقَيْنَاهُم مَّاءً غَدَقًا
لِنَفْتِنَهُمْ فِيهِ وَمَن يُعْرِضْ عَن ذِكْرِ رَبِّهِ يَسْلُكْهُ عَذَابًا صَعَدًا
إِنَّا إِلَى رَبِّنَا لَمُنقَلِبُونَ

Di: "Solo invoco a mi Señor y no asocio a nadie
con Él."
Y di: "No soy en absoluto un guardián sobre
vosotros."
Ni soy responsable de lo que hacéis.
Y [di]: "Ciertamente, cuando esté con mi Señor, seré
devuelto a Él."

Say, "I only invoke my Lord and do not associate with Him
anyone."
And say, "I am not at all a guardian over you."

Nor am I responsible for what you do.
And [say], "Indeed, when I am with my Lord, I will be
brought back to Him."

SURAH 72, VERSOS 154, 155 Y 156

وَلَا تَقُولُوا لِمَن يُقْتَلُ فِي سَبِيلِ اللهِ أَمْوَاتٌ ۚ بَلْ أَحْيَاءٌ وَلَٰكِن لَّا تَشْعُرُونَ
وَلَنَبْلُوَنَّكُم بِشَيْءٍ مِّنَ الْخَوْفِ وَالْجُوعِ وَنَقْصٍ مِّنَ الْأَمْوَالِ وَالْأَنفُسِ
وَالثَّمَرَاتِ ۗ وَبَشِّرِ الصَّابِرِينَ
الَّذِينَ إِذَا أَصَابَتْهُم مُّصِيبَةٌ قَالُوا إِنَّا لِلَّهِ وَإِنَّا إِلَيْهِ رَاجِعُونَ

Y no digáis de los que caen por Dios que están
muertos. No, están vivos, aunque vosotros no lo
percibáis.

Seguramente os probaremos con algo de miedo,
hambre y pérdida de bienes, vidas y frutos. Pero da
buenas noticias a los pacientes,

quienes cuando les alcanza una desgracia, dicen:
"Ciertamente, a Dios pertenecemos y a Él hemos de
regresar".

And do not say about those who are killed in the way of

Allah, "They are dead." Rather, they are alive, but you
perceive [it] not.
And We will surely test you with something of fear and
hunger and a loss of wealth and lives and fruits, but give
good tidings to the patient,
Who, when disaster strikes them, say, "Indeed we belong to
Allah, and indeed to Him we will return."

SURAH 74, VERSOS 42, 43, 44, 45, 46 Y 47

مَا سَلَكَكُمْ فِي سَقَرَ
قَالُوا لَمْ نَكُ مِنَ الْمُصَلِّينَ
وَلَمْ نَكُ نُطْعِمُ الْمِسْكِينَ
وَكُنَّا نَخُوضُ مَعَ الْخَائِضِينَ
وَكُنَّا نُكَذِّبُ بِيَوْمِ الدِّينِ
حَتَّىٰ أَتَانَا الْيَقِينُ

"¿Qué os ha llevado a Saqar?
Dirán: "No éramos de los que oraban,
ni alimentábamos al pobre,
y solíamos hablar vanidades con los que lo hacían,
y negábamos el Día del Juicio,
hasta que nos llegó la certeza (la muerte)."

"What has brought you into Hell-fire?"
They will say, "We were not of those who prayed,

nor did we use to feed the poor.
And we used to enter into vain discourse with those who
engaged [in it],
and we used to deny the Day of Recompense
until there came to us the certainty."

Surah 18, Versos 109 y 110

قُل لَّوْ كَانَ الْبَحْرُ مِدَادًا لِّكَلِمَاتِ رَبِّي لَنَفِدَ الْبَحْرُ قَبْلَ أَن تَنفَدَ كَلِمَاتُ
رَبِّي وَلَوْ جِئْنَا بِمِثْلِهِ مَدَدًا
قُلْ إِنَّمَا أَنَا بَشَرٌ مِّثْلُكُمْ يُوحَىٰ إِلَيَّ أَنَّمَا إِلَٰهُكُمْ إِلَٰهٌ وَاحِدٌ فَمَن كَانَ يَرْجُو
لِقَاءَ رَبِّهِ فَلْيَعْمَلْ عَمَلًا صَالِحًا وَلَا يُشْرِكْ بِعِبَادَةِ رَبِّهِ أَحَدًا

Di: "Si el mar fuera tinta para escribir las palabras de
mi Señor, se agotaría el mar antes de que se agotaran
las palabras de mi Señor, aun si trajéramos otro tanto
para auxiliarlo".

Di: "Soy sólo un ser humano como vosotros, a quien se
le ha revelado que vuestro dios es un único Dios. Así
que, quien espere encontrar a su Señor, que haga
buenas obras y que no asocie a nadie en la adoración
de su Señor".

Say, "If the sea were ink for [writing] the words of my Lord,

the sea would be exhausted before the words of my Lord were
exhausted, even if We brought the like of it as a supplement."
Say, "I am only a human being like you, to whom it has been
revealed that your god is one God. So whoever hopes for the
meeting with his Lord, let him do righteous work and not
associate in the worship of his Lord anyone."

SURAH 71, VERSOS 10, 11 Y 12

قُلْتُ اسْتَغْفِرُوا رَبَّكُمْ إِنَّهُ كَانَ غَفَّارًا

يُرْسِلِ السَّمَاءَ عَلَيْكُم مِّدْرَارًا

وَيُمْدِدْكُم بِأَمْوَالٍ وَبَنِينَ وَيَجْعَل لَّكُمْ جَنَّاتٍ وَيَجْعَل لَّكُمْ أَنْهَارًا

Dije: 'Pedid perdón a vuestro Señor. Realmente, Él es siempre Perdonador.
Él enviará del cielo sobre vosotros lluvias abundantes, y os aumentará vuestras riquezas y vuestros hijos, y os hará jardines y os hará ríos.

I said, 'Ask forgiveness of your Lord. Indeed, He is ever a Perpetual Forgiver.
He will send [rain from] the sky upon you in [continuing] showers
And give you increase in wealth and children and provide for you gardens and provide for you rivers.

SURAH 89, VERSOS 27, 28, 29 Y 30

يَا أَيَّتُهَا النَّفْسُ الْمُطْمَئِنَّةُ
ارْجِعِي إِلَىٰ رَبِّكِ رَاضِيَةً مَرْضِيَّةً
فَادْخُلِي فِي عِبَادِي
وَادْخُلِي جَنَّتِي

¡Oh alma serena!
Vuelve a tu Señor, complacida y complaciente.
Entra, pues, entre Mis siervos,
Entra en Mi jardín.

O, tranquil soul!
Return to your Lord, well-pleased and pleasing [to Him],
And enter among My [righteous] servants
And enter My Paradise.

O Lord of the whole universe! Forgive us all our sins without reckoning without punishment with your grace and mercy and purify us and the hearts and souls of our generations until the Day of Resurrection.

Protect us and the hearts and souls of our generations from Satan until the Day of Resurrection.

O Holy Lord of all the worlds! Fill the lives and homes of us and our generations with your mercy and grace until the Day of Judgement.

O Holy Lord of all the worlds! Fill the lives and homes of us and our generations with faith and guidance until the Day of Resurrection.

O Holy Lord of all the worlds! May the lives and homes of us and our generations be filled with health, blessings and peace til the Day of Judgement, Amen.

Printed in the United States
by Baker & Taylor Publisher Services